CONTENTS

NOTE: Whenever a numerical value of g is required, use $g = 9.8 \text{ m s}^{-2}$

Uniform Acceleration

Exercise 1S   Skills Practice

1   In each part of this question a particle moves in a straight line with constant acceleration a ms^{-2}. It passes a point O with velocity u ms^{-1} and t seconds later it has velocity v ms^{-1} and its displacement from O is s metres.

    a $u = 4,\ a = 2,\ t = 3$; find v.   **b** $u = 5,\ v = 9,\ t = 3$; find s.

    c $u = 0,\ a = 3,\ s = 6$; find v.   **d** $u = 18,\ a = -2,\ t = 5$; find s.

    e $u = 7.3,\ a = 2.4,\ t = 6.5$; find v.   **f** $u = 2.6,\ a = 4,\ s = 2.8$; find v.

2   A particle moving in a straight line accelerates uniformly from 3 ms^{-1} to 7 ms^{-1} over 12 seconds. Find the distance travelled by the particle during this period.

3   A cyclist is travelling at 15.2 ms^{-1} on a straight road. She then applies the brakes producing a constant retardation of 3.4 ms^{-2}.

Find her speed 2 seconds after she starts braking.

4   In each part of this question a particle moves in a straight line with constant acceleration a ms^{-2}. It passes a point O with velocity u ms^{-1} and t seconds later it has velocity v ms^{-1} and its displacement from O is s metres.

    a $u = 12,\ v = 0,\ s = 24$; find a.   **b** $v = 18,\ t = 10,\ s = 140$; find u.

    c $u = 25,\ v = 7,\ a = -3$; find t.   **d** $u = 0,\ a = 10,\ s = 125$; find t.

    e $a = 1,\ t = 4,\ v = 9$; find s.   **f** $u = 7,\ a = -2,\ s = 0$; find t.

5   A particle moving along a straight line accelerates uniformly from 2.1 ms^{-1} to 15.7 ms^{-1} over 4 seconds. Find the acceleration of the particle.

6   A car moving along a straight road at 25 ms^{-1} decelerates uniformly at 3 ms^{-2} until its speed is 7 ms^{-1}. Find the distance travelled by the car during this period.

7   A car accelerates uniformly from rest at 4 ms^{-2} along a straight track until it reaches a speed of 18 ms^{-1}. Find how long this takes and the distance the car travels in this time.

8   A van travelling at 54 kmh^{-1} increases its speed to 72 kmh^{-1} over 10 seconds.

    a Express 54 kmh^{-1} in ms^{-1}.

Assuming that the van moves in a straight line and its acceleration is uniform,

    b find its acceleration in ms^{-2},

    c find the distance travelled by the van as it accelerates.

The Advanced Study Series

M1 Improving Skills

by
Shaun Armstrong, Chris Huffer and Craig Hunter

Solomon Press

Published by Solomon Press
3 Dunkirk Business Park, Frome Road, Southwick,
Wiltshire, BA14 9NL

Tel: 01225 775 078
E-mail: info@solomon-press.com
Website: www.solomon-press.com

The *Advanced Study Series* is a trade mark of Solomon Press

© S Armstrong C Huffer C Hunter 2002
First published 2002

ISBN 1901724298

Design and typesetting by S Armstrong and Solomon Press Ltd.
Printed in Great Britain by S & G Print Group, Merthyr Tydfil, Wales.

9   A passenger train requires 1200 metres of straight track to decelerate uniformly to rest from its maximum speed of 60 ms^{-1}. Calculate the magnitude of the train's deceleration and find how long it takes to come to a halt.

10   A car is travelling at 25 ms^{-1} on a straight road when the driver sees that the traffic ahead is stationary. The driver begins braking at a distance of 48 metres from the first stationary vehicle, producing a uniform retardation of 6 ms^{-2}.

  a   Find the speed with which the car hits the stationary vehicle.

  b   Find the maximum speed at which the car could have been travelling such that the driver could have stopped without hitting the stationary vehicle.

11   A goods train accelerates uniformly from rest on a straight track for $1\frac{1}{2}$ minutes, travelling a distance of 729 metres. It then maintains the speed it has reached for a further 10 minutes.

  Find the acceleration of the train and the total distance it travels in $11\frac{1}{2}$ minutes.

12   A particle P passes the point O with velocity 7 ms^{-1} and moves in a straight line with constant acceleration -4 ms^{-2} until it returns to O.

  a   Given that P is 5 m from O at time t seconds after passing O, show that t satisfies the equation $2t^2 - 7t + 5 = 0$.

  b   Hence find for how long P is more than 5 metres from O.

13   A motorbike accelerating at a constant rate a ms^{-2} along a straight road passes the point O at u ms^{-1}. Three seconds later the motorbike passes the point A, 24 metres from O, and after a further 2 seconds it passes the point B, 26 metres from A.

  a   By considering the journey OA, show that $2u + 3a = 16$.

  b   Find and simplify a similar equation for the journey OB.

  c   Hence find u and a.

14   A car is travelling along a straight road. It begins to decelerate uniformly at the point O and passes through the point A, 28 metres from O, and the point B, 60 metres from A, before coming to rest at the point C. The car takes 1 second to travel from O to A and 3 seconds to travel from A to B.

  a   Find the deceleration of the car.

  b   Find the velocity of the car at O.

  c   Find the time taken for the car to travel from B to C.

  d   Find the distance OC.

Exercise 1E   Exam Practice

1   A drag racer travelling with uniform acceleration on a straight track passes three checkpoints. It takes 2 seconds to travel the 26 metres between the first two checkpoints and 5 seconds to travel the 170 metres between the second and third checkpoints.

    a   Find the acceleration of the racer.   **(6 marks)**

    b   Find the velocity of the racer as it passes the second checkpoint.   **(3 marks)**

2   Two particles, A and B, are at rest a distance x m apart. At the same time the particles begin to move in the same direction and such that A is moving directly towards B.

    Given that A and B accelerate uniformly at 5 ms^{-2} and 2 ms^{-2} respectively, and they collide when B has travelled 100 metres, find the value of x and the speed of A at the time of collision.   **(7 marks)**

3   A particle P accelerates uniformly from 2 ms^{-1} to 20 ms^{-1} over a period of T seconds. During the same time period another particle, Q, accelerates uniformly at 1 ms^{-2} from an initial speed of 4.5 ms^{-1}.

    Given that during this period both particles travel a distance of S metres find the values of S and T.   **(6 marks)**

4   A car travels along a straight road with constant velocity 61.2 kmh^{-1}. When the car's brakes are applied to greatest effect they can produce a constant retardation of 6 ms^{-2}. The driver of the car misjudges a red light and begins to brake 0.5 seconds too late to stop at the lights.

    a   Find the speed of the car as it passes the lights.   **(6 marks)**

    b   Find the distance by which the car overshoots the lights.   **(2 marks)**

5   Two toy cars A and B move in the same direction along a straight line. Initially the cars are 56 m apart with car A in front travelling at 10 ms^{-1} and car B travelling behind at 18 ms^{-1}. Both cars then experience uniform retardation of 0.5 ms^{-2} until they collide.

    a   Find the time which elapses before the cars collide.   **(6 marks)**

    b   Find the distance travelled before the collision by car B.   **(2 marks)**

6   A cyclist riding along a straight road accelerates uniformly from 4 ms^{-1} to 9 ms^{-1} over 8 seconds.

    a   Find how far the cyclist travels while accelerating.   **(2 marks)**

    b   Find, to 3 significant figures, the length of time it takes the cyclist to cover the first half of this distance.   **(7 marks)**

Motion / time Graphs

Exercise 2S   Skills Practice

1 A man takes 15 minutes to walk at constant speed along a straight road from his home to a grocery store 1.5 km away. He spends 7 minutes in the shop before returning home at constant speed in 18 minutes.

    a Sketch a displacement-time graph for this period.

    b Find the man's speed in kmh^{-1} as he walks to the shop.

    c Find the man's average speed in kmh^{-1} during this 40 minute period.

2

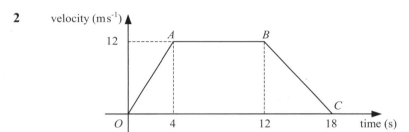

The velocity-time graph shows the motion of a particle along a straight line.

    a Find the acceleration during OA.

    b Find the deceleration during BC.

    c Find the total distance travelled by the particle.

3 A girl kicks a football so that it strikes a wall 8 m away at right angles. The ball travels to the wall at a constant speed of $16\ ms^{-1}$ and returns along the same path at a constant speed of $12\ ms^{-1}$. The girl then stops the ball at a distance of 6 m from the wall.

    a Draw a displacement-time graph for the motion of the ball where the displacement is measured from the point at which it was kicked.

    b Find the average speed of the ball while it is moving.

    c Find the average velocity of the ball while it is moving.

4 A lorry passes the point A on a straight road at a constant speed of $18\ ms^{-1}$ and maintains this speed for 5 seconds. The driver of the lorry then applies the brakes and the lorry decelerates uniformly to rest at the point B.

    a Sketch the speed-time graph for the lorry's journey from A to B.

    Given that $AB = 117$ m,

    b find the length of time it takes the lorry to stop once the brakes are applied,

    c find the retardation of the lorry.

5   A motorbike starts from rest at a set of traffic lights and moves along a straight road with constant acceleration 4 ms^{-2} until it reaches a speed of 20 ms^{-1}. It maintains this speed for 36 seconds before decelerating at 5 ms^{-2} until it comes to rest at the next set of traffic lights.

    a Draw a speed-time graph to show the motion of the motorbike.

    b Find the distance between the two sets of traffic lights.

    c Find the motorbike's average speed for the whole journey.

6

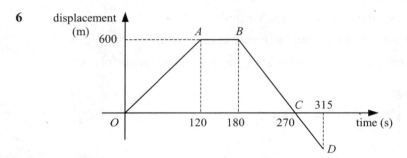

The displacement-time graph shows a cycle journey along a straight road.

    a Describe the journey for the period shown.

    b Find the cyclist's speed during OA.

Given that the cyclist maintained a constant velocity during BD,

    c find the final displacement of the cyclist,

    d find the cyclist's average speed for the whole journey correct to 2 sf.

7   In a 100 m race on a straight track a sprinter accelerates uniformly from rest to a top speed of V ms^{-1} in 2 seconds. He maintains this speed until he crosses the finishing line 8.5 seconds later and then decelerates to rest uniformly in 4 seconds.

    a Sketch a speed-time graph to show the sprinter's motion.

    b Find V correct to 3 sf.

    c Find the total distance travelled by the sprinter correct to 3 sf.

8   A car is travels along a straight road at a constant speed of 40 ms^{-1}. At the instant the car passes a police motorcyclist at rest, the motorcyclist sets off in pursuit. The motorcyclist accelerates at 3 ms^{-2} for 15 seconds before travelling at constant velocity until it catches the car T seconds after setting off.

    a Sketch a velocity-time graph showing the motion of both vehicles.

    b Find the value of T.

    c Find the distance the motorcyclist travels before catching the car.

Exercise 2E   Exam Practice

1   A car moving along a straight road decelerates uniformly from 16 ms^{-1} for 5 seconds. The car then maintains constant velocity for 15 seconds before accelerating uniformly back up to 16 ms^{-1} in 5 seconds.

   a   Sketch a speed-time graph to illustrate the car's motion.   **(2 marks)**

   Given that the car travels a total distance of 300 m in this time,

   b   find the constant velocity which was maintained for 15 seconds.   **(4 marks)**

2   Mark and Steve cycle along a straight road from college to a shop.

   Mark accelerates uniformly from rest to a speed of 7 ms^{-1} over 20 seconds. He then maintains this speed for 3 minutes before decelerating uniformly to rest over 30 seconds. Steve sets off 40 seconds after Mark and accelerates uniformly for 15 seconds. He then maintains constant speed before decelerating uniformly to rest over 10 seconds, arriving at the shop at the same time as Mark.

   a   Sketch on the same diagram speed-time graphs for both cyclists.   **(4 marks)**

   b   Find Steve's initial acceleration correct to 2 significant figures.   **(6 marks)**

3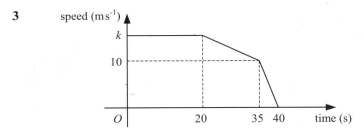

   The speed-time graph above illustrates part of a car's journey.

   The car travels along a straight road at $k \text{ ms}^{-1}$ for 20 seconds before uniformly decelerating to 10 ms^{-1} over 15 seconds. The car then uniformly decelerates to rest over a further 5 seconds

   a   Find the magnitude of the car's final deceleration.   **(2 marks)**

   Given that the car travels 540 metres during this part of its journey,

   b   find the value of k.   **(5 marks)**

4   A particle moving on a straight line accelerates uniformly from rest at 2 ms^{-2} for 8 seconds. It then decelerates uniformly at 0.5 ms^{-2} for 14 seconds before travelling at constant speed for 5 seconds. The particle then decelerates uniformly to rest in 6 seconds.

   a   Illustrate the particle's motion on a speed-time graph.   **(3 marks)**

   b   Find the magnitude of the particle's final deceleration.   **(4 marks)**

   c   Find the total distance travelled by the particle.   **(4 marks)**

Vertical Motion

Exercise 3S   Skills Practice

1   A tile falls from the roof of a garage which is 2.5 metres high.

Find the speed with which the tile hits the ground.

2   A rock falls from a cliff face and moves freely until it hits the sea 60 m below.

Find how long it takes the rock to reach the sea in seconds correct to 1 dp.

3   A student wants to estimate the height of a school building. He drops a coin from the top of the building and notes that it takes 1.8 seconds to reach the ground.

a   Suggest, with a reason, a suitable model for the coin.

b   Find an estimate for the height of the building correct to the nearest metre.

In fact, the building is 15 metres high.

c   Suggest why your answer to part **b** is more than 15 metres.

4   A ball is thrown vertically upwards with speed 14 ms^{-1}.

Find the greatest height reached by the ball above the point of projection.

5   A girl uses a tennis racket to hit a ball vertically upwards. Find the minimum initial speed she must give the ball for it to reach a height of 40 metres above the point at which the racket hits the ball.

6   A particle is projected vertically upwards at 24 ms^{-1} from a point 2.5 m above the ground.

a   Find to 2 sf how long it takes to reach its maximum height.

b   Find the speed with which it hits the ground.

7   A rocket is projected vertically upwards with speed 117.6 ms^{-1}. Modelling the rocket as a particle and ignoring air resistance,

a   find to 2 sf the height of the rocket when its speed has dropped to 78.4 ms^{-1},

b   find for how long the rocket is above this height.

8   A particle is dropped from rest at a height of 12 metres above the ground. At the same instant that another particle is projected vertically upwards from the ground with speed 15 ms^{-1}.

Given that the two particles collide, find correct to 2 sf the height above the ground at which this happens.

Exercise 3E   Exam Practice

1   A marble is projected vertically upwards with an initial velocity of 19.6 ms^{-1}.

    a Find the length of time for which the marble is more than 14.7 m above the point of projection. **(5 marks)**

    b State the modelling assumptions used in your calculation. **(2 marks)**

2   A ball is thrown vertically upwards with velocity 39.2 ms^{-1}.

Find for how long the speed of the ball is less than 24.5 ms^{-1}. **(5 marks)**

3   A power ball is dropped from a height of 15.625 m above a horizontal plane. Given that the speed of the ball is instantaneously reduced by 20% each time it bounces, show that the maximum height reached by the ball after its third bounce is 4.1 m correct to 2 significant figures. **(8 marks)**

4   Two particles, P and Q, are projected vertically upwards at the same time with velocities v_P ms^{-1} and v_Q ms^{-1} respectively, where $v_P > v_Q$.

Show that if the particles are allowed to move freely under gravity the time difference between the first bounce of the particles is given by $\frac{2(v_P - v_Q)}{g}$ seconds. **(6 marks)**

5   A particle is projected vertically upwards from ground level with speed u ms^{-1} and moves freely under gravity.

    a Show that the particle returns to ground level with speed u ms^{-1}. **(2 marks)**

A ball is dropped from a height of 20 m above a horizontal plane. Given that each time the ball bounces its speed is instantaneously halved,

    b find, to an appropriate degree of accuracy, the total time for which the ball is more than 4 m above the horizontal plane. **(9 marks)**

6   Two particles, A and B, are projected vertically upwards from the same horizontal plane. Given that the maximum height above the plane reached by B is four times that reached by A, find the ratio of the initial velocity of A to the initial velocity of B. **(6 marks)**

7   A parachutist drops vertically from a helicopter hovering 500 m above the ground. She free-falls for 3 seconds then the parachute opens causing her to decelerate at 12 ms^{-2} for 2 seconds before reaching constant velocity.

Find, to the nearest second, how long it takes the parachutist to fall from the helicopter to the ground. **(9 marks)**

Kinematics Review

Exercise 4E   Exam Practice

1   A boy leans out of a window 15 metres above the ground and throws
a ball vertically upwards with initial velocity 21.5 ms^{-1}.

Modelling the ball as a particle and ignoring air resistance, find how
long it takes for the ball to hit the ground.   **(5 marks)**

2   A motorbike moving along a straight road with constant acceleration
passes the point P at 16 ms^{-1}. Five seconds later it passes the point Q
and after a further 5 seconds it passes the point R.

Given that $PR = 220$ metres,

   a find the acceleration of the motorbike,   **(3 marks)**

   b find the ratio of the distances $PQ : QR$ in its simplest form.   **(4 marks)**

3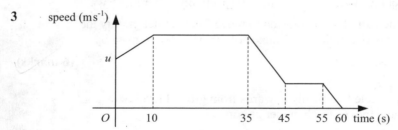

The speed-time graph above illustrates part of a car journey along a
straight road. From its initial speed, u, the car accelerates uniformly
for 10 seconds until its speed is 50% greater than u. It maintains this
speed for 25 seconds then decelerates uniformly over 10 seconds until
its speed is 50% less than u. The car then continues at this speed for
10 seconds before decelerating uniformly to rest in a further 5 seconds.

   a Show that the magnitude of the deceleration was the same each
time the car slowed down.   **(4 marks)**

Given that the car travelled 1.2 km during the first 35 seconds of
this part of its journey,

   b find u.   **(4 marks)**

4   A ball is thrown vertically upwards with initial speed 29.4 ms^{-1}.
Two seconds later another ball is thrown vertically upwards with
the same initial speed.

   a Find for how long the first ball is in motion before the two balls
are at the same height.   **(5 marks)**

   b Find the height of the balls at this time to an appropriate degree
of accuracy.   **(2 marks)**

5 Particle P has initial velocity u and accelerates uniformly until it has velocity 15 ms^{-1}. During this period of acceleration P travels a distance of 90 m.

Particle Q has initial velocity $2u$. It accelerates uniformly at 0.75 ms^{-2} and takes 2 seconds longer than P to reach a velocity of 15 ms^{-1}.

Given that as they accelerate both particles move in the same direction along a straight line, find u.   **(9 marks)**

6   velocity (ms^{-1})

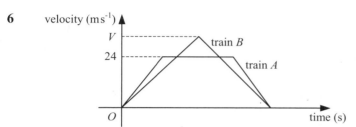

The velocity-time graph above shows the motion of two underground trains travelling on a straight track between two stations 1.8 km apart.

Train A accelerates uniformly from rest for 480 m until it reaches 24 ms^{-1}. It then maintains this speed for T seconds before decelerating uniformly at 1.2 ms^{-2} until it comes to rest.

a   Find the acceleration of train A over the first 480 m of travel.   **(3 marks)**

b   Find T.   **(4 marks)**

Train B completes the journey in the same time by accelerating uniformly from rest to reach speed V ms^{-1} and then immediately decelerating uniformly to rest.

c   Find V correct to 3 significant figures.   **(5 marks)**

7 In a scene for a film, two cars P and Q are required to perform a head-on collision. Initially, the cars are 495 m apart and travelling towards each other with P having speed 7 ms^{-1} and Q having speed 5 ms^{-1}. Given that P and Q travel towards each other on a straight road with uniform accelerations of 1.2 ms^{-2} and 1.6 ms^{-2} respectively, find how long it takes for the cars to collide.   **(7 marks)**

8 A particle moves uniformly on a horizontal plane. It passes through the points A, B and C at times $t = 0$, $t = 3$ and $t = 8$ seconds respectively. The distance AB is 198 m and the distance BC is 210 m.

a   Find the acceleration of the particle and the speed at which it passes through the point A.   **(6 marks)**

b   Sketch a velocity-time graph to illustrate the motion of the particle in the time interval $0 \leq t \leq 20$.   **(3 marks)**

c   Find the total distance travelled by the particle from when it passes through A at $t = 0$ until it returns to the point A.   **(4 marks)**

9   **a**   Show that an acceleration of 1 ms^{-2} is equivalent to 12 960 kmh^{-2}.   **(2 marks)**

In a computer simulation, two trains A and B are placed 3.6 km apart, facing each other. At the same time both trains begin to accelerate uniformly from rest directly towards each other such that they collide with each train having speed 108 kmh^{-1}.

   b   Find the length of time for which the trains were in motion before colliding.   **(4 marks)**

   c   Find the acceleration, in kmh^{-2}, of the trains whilst they were in motion.   **(3 marks)**

   d   Express the acceleration of the trains in ms^{-2}.   **(1 mark)**

10   Habib wishes to check the engine in his car by listening for odd noises as he drives along a straight road. For his trial, he begins from rest and accelerates uniformly at 1 ms^{-2} before maintaining a speed of 5 ms^{-1} for T seconds. He repeats his acceleration and maintains speeds of 10 ms^{-1}, 15 ms^{-1} and 20 ms^{-1} for T seconds each before finally decelerating uniformly to rest in 8 seconds.

   a   Illustrate his test journey on a speed-time graph.   **(3 marks)**

   b   Given that he travelled a total distance of 580 m, find T.   **(6 marks)**

11   Two fireworks are projected vertically upwards at the same time from the same horizontal level. One is projected with velocity 29.4 ms^{-1}, whilst the other has initial velocity 24.5 ms^{-1}. Find the time difference between the fireworks returning to the horizontal level of projection.   **(5 marks)**

12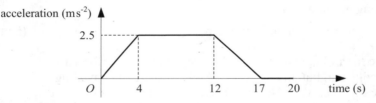

The acceleration-time graph above illustrates part of a car journey along a straight road. The car accelerates from rest at time $t = 0$ seconds and maintains a constant acceleration of 2.5 ms^{-2} in the interval $4 \le t \le 12$. In the interval $17 \le t \le 20$, the car's acceleration is 0.

Given that when $t = 4$ the car's speed is 5 ms^{-1},

   a   find how far the car travels in the interval $4 \le t \le 12$.   **(3 marks)**

   b   Sketch a speed-time graph for the car's motion in the interval $0 \le t \le 20$.   **(4 marks)**

Vectors

Exercise 5S   Skills Practice

1

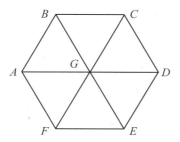

The diagram above shows a hexagon made up of 6 equilateral triangles. Given that **m** = $\overrightarrow{AB}$ and **n** = $\overrightarrow{AF}$, express the following vectors in terms of **m** and **n**.

  a $\overrightarrow{GC}$ **b** $\overrightarrow{BE}$ **c** $\overrightarrow{AG}$ **d** $\overrightarrow{AE}$ **e** $\overrightarrow{DC}$ **f** $\overrightarrow{FB}$

2

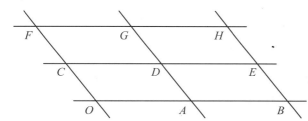

The diagram above shows two sets of equally-spaced parallel lines. Given that **p** = $\overrightarrow{OA}$ and **q** = $\overrightarrow{OF}$, express the following vectors in terms of **p** and **q**.

  a $\overrightarrow{OB}$ **b** $\overrightarrow{OC}$ **c** $\overrightarrow{OG}$ **d** $\overrightarrow{OD}$ **e** $\overrightarrow{EC}$ **f** $\overrightarrow{EB}$

  g $\overrightarrow{HA}$ **h** $\overrightarrow{AF}$ **i** $\overrightarrow{CH}$ **j** $\overrightarrow{GE}$ **k** $\overrightarrow{FB}$ **l** $\overrightarrow{BC}$

3   In each part of this question find the magnitude and direction of the displacement vector $\overrightarrow{OQ}$. Give the direction as a bearing to the nearest degree and where appropriate give the magnitude correct to 3 sf.

  a   The point P is 48 km due north of the point O.
      The point Q is 14 km due east of the point P.

  b   The point P is 400 km due west of the point O.
      The point Q is 50 km due south of the point P.

  c   The point P is 35 m south-east of the point O.
      The point Q is 20 m due east of the point P.

  d   The point P is 6 km from the point O on a bearing of 032°.
      The point Q is 8 km from the point P on a bearing of 085°.

In questions 4 to 12, **i** and **j** are perpendicular unit vectors.

4   Given that $\mathbf{u} = 3\mathbf{i} + 2\mathbf{j}$ and $\mathbf{v} = 4\mathbf{i} - \mathbf{j}$, find in terms of **i** and **j**

    a $2\mathbf{u}$ **b** $\mathbf{u} + \mathbf{v}$ **c** $3\mathbf{u} + 2\mathbf{v}$ **d** $-2\mathbf{u} + 5\mathbf{v}$

5   Find the magnitude of each of the following vectors giving your answers to 3 sf where appropriate.

    a $4\mathbf{i} - 3\mathbf{j}$ **b** $5\mathbf{i} + 12\mathbf{j}$ **c** $-6\mathbf{i} + \mathbf{j}$ **d** $-2\mathbf{i} - 11\mathbf{j}$

6   Given that $\mathbf{m} = 8\mathbf{i} + t\mathbf{j}$ and that the magnitude of **m** is 17, find the two possible values of t.

7   Find, in degrees to 1 dp, the acute angle made with the vector **i** by each of the following vectors:

    a $\mathbf{i} + \mathbf{j}$ **b** $6\mathbf{i} + 4\mathbf{j}$ **c** $9\mathbf{i} - \mathbf{j}$ **d** $3\mathbf{i} + 7\mathbf{j}$

8   Find in the form $\lambda\mathbf{i} + \mu\mathbf{j}$,

    a a vector of magnitude 20 in the direction of the vector $3\mathbf{i} - 4\mathbf{j}$,

    b a vector of magnitude 5 in the direction of the vector $7\mathbf{i} + 24\mathbf{j}$.

9   Find in exact form a unit vector in the direction

    a $6\mathbf{i} + 8\mathbf{j}$ · **b** $7\mathbf{i} - 24\mathbf{j}$ **c** $\mathbf{i} + \mathbf{j}$ **d** $-2\mathbf{i} + 4\mathbf{j}$

10   Given that the vector $3\mathbf{i} + k\mathbf{j}$ is parallel to the vector $9\mathbf{i} + 15\mathbf{j}$, find k.

11   Given that $\mathbf{m} = 2\mathbf{i} + \mathbf{j}$ and $\mathbf{n} = \mathbf{i} - 3\mathbf{j}$, find the values of s and t for which

    a $\mathbf{m} + s\mathbf{n}$ is parallel to the vector **i**,

    b $t\mathbf{m} + \mathbf{n}$ is parallel to the vector **j**.

12   Given that $\mathbf{p} = 4\mathbf{i} - \mathbf{j}$ and $\mathbf{q} = 2\mathbf{i} + 3\mathbf{j}$, find the values of u and v for which

    a $\mathbf{p} + u\mathbf{q}$ is parallel to the vector $\mathbf{i} + \mathbf{j}$,

    b $v\mathbf{p} + \mathbf{q}$ is parallel to the vector $\mathbf{i} + 2\mathbf{j}$.

13   Taking **i** and **j** as unit vectors due east and due north respectively, find in the form $a\mathbf{i} + b\mathbf{j}$, where a and b are exact

    a a vector of magnitude 10 on a bearing of $060°$,

    b a vector of magnitude 5 on a bearing of $270°$,

    c a vector of magnitude 16 on a bearing of $135°$,

    d a vector of magnitude 30 on a bearing of $210°$.

Applications of Vectors

Exercise 6S   Skills Practice

In this exercise **i** and **j** are unit vectors in the direction of the positive x and y-axes respectively unless otherwise stated.

1   Find in the form $(a\mathbf{i} + b\mathbf{j})$ the velocity of

    a   a particle moving with speed 4 ms^{-1} parallel to the positive x-axis,

    b   a particle moving with speed 15 ms^{-1} parallel to the vector $(3\mathbf{i} - 4\mathbf{j})$,

    c   a particle moving with speed 6.5 ms^{-1} along the line from the point with position vector $(3\mathbf{i} - 4\mathbf{j})$ to the point with position vector $(-2\mathbf{i} + 8\mathbf{j})$.

2   A particle is at the point with position vector **r** m. It moves with constant velocity **v** ms^{-1} and after t seconds it is at the point with position vector **s** m.

    Find **v** when

    a $\mathbf{r} = 2\mathbf{i}$, $\mathbf{s} = 8\mathbf{i}$, $t = 2$ **b** $\mathbf{r} = \mathbf{j}$, $\mathbf{s} = 10\mathbf{i} - 4\mathbf{j}$, $t = 5$

    c $\mathbf{r} = 3\mathbf{i} + \mathbf{j}$, $\mathbf{s} = 6\mathbf{i} + 13\mathbf{j}$, $t = 3$ **d** $\mathbf{r} = 6\mathbf{i} - 4\mathbf{j}$, $\mathbf{s} = 10\mathbf{i} + 2\mathbf{j}$, $t = 2$

    e $\mathbf{r} = 5\mathbf{i} - \mathbf{j}$, $\mathbf{s} = -3\mathbf{i} - 17\mathbf{j}$, $t = 4$ **f** $\mathbf{r} = -5\mathbf{i} - 7\mathbf{j}$, $\mathbf{s} = \mathbf{i} + 4\mathbf{j}$, $t = 2$

3   At time $t = 0$ a particle at the point with position vector $(3\mathbf{i} + 2\mathbf{j})$ m begins moving with constant velocity. Given that at time $t = 3$ seconds the particle passes through the point with position vector $(9\mathbf{i} - 7\mathbf{j})$ m, find its speed correct to 3 sf.

4   A particle moves with constant velocity from the point with position vector $(-3\mathbf{i} + 6\mathbf{j})$ m to the point with position vector $(\mathbf{i} - 4\mathbf{j})$ m in 2 seconds.

    a   Find the speed of the particle correct to 3 sf.

    b   Find, to the nearest degree, the angle the particle's velocity makes with the vector **i**.

5   A particle at the origin O begins to move with constant velocity $(2\mathbf{i} + \mathbf{j})$ ms^{-1}.

    Find the position vector of the particle 3 seconds later.

6   A particle is at the point with position vector **r** m. It moves with constant velocity **v** ms^{-1} and after t seconds it is at the point with position vector **s** m.

    Find **s** when

    a $\mathbf{r} = 3\mathbf{j}$, $\mathbf{v} = 2\mathbf{i} + \mathbf{j}$, $t = 1$ **b** $\mathbf{r} = 5\mathbf{i}$, $\mathbf{v} = -2\mathbf{j}$, $t = 2$

    c $\mathbf{r} = 2\mathbf{i}$, $\mathbf{v} = \mathbf{i} + \mathbf{j}$, $t = 6$ **d** $\mathbf{r} = -\mathbf{i} + 2\mathbf{j}$, $\mathbf{v} = 2\mathbf{i} + \mathbf{j}$, $t = 3$

    e $\mathbf{r} = 3\mathbf{i} + 5\mathbf{j}$, $\mathbf{v} = 2\mathbf{i} - \mathbf{j}$, $t = 2$ **f** $\mathbf{r} = 3\mathbf{i} - 2\mathbf{j}$, $\mathbf{v} = -\mathbf{i} + \frac{1}{2}\mathbf{j}$, $t = 4$

7   A particle moves with speed 2.5 ms^{-1} parallel to the vector $(4\mathbf{i} - 3\mathbf{j})$. Find the position vector of the particle 6 seconds after it passes through the origin O.

8   A particle moves with uniform velocity and passes through the point with position vector $(7\mathbf{i} - 4\mathbf{j})$ m. Three seconds later the particle passes through the point with position vector $(-2\mathbf{i} + 2\mathbf{j})$ m. Find the position vector of the particle after a further 5 seconds.

9   A particle has initial velocity $\mathbf{u}$ ms^{-1}. The particle moves with uniform acceleration $\mathbf{a}$ ms^{-2} and after t seconds it has velocity $\mathbf{v}$ ms^{-1}.

Find $\mathbf{a}$ when

a $\mathbf{u} = 2\mathbf{i}$, $\mathbf{v} = 3\mathbf{i}$, $t = 2$ b $\mathbf{u} = 3\mathbf{i}$, $\mathbf{v} = 3\mathbf{i} + 8\mathbf{j}$, $t = 4$

c $\mathbf{u} = 2\mathbf{j}$, $\mathbf{v} = 2\mathbf{i} - 2\mathbf{j}$, $t = 2$ d $\mathbf{u} = \mathbf{i} + \mathbf{j}$, $\mathbf{v} = 10\mathbf{i} - 5\mathbf{j}$, $t = 3$

e $\mathbf{u} = 5\mathbf{i} - 2\mathbf{j}$, $\mathbf{v} = -\mathbf{i} + 4\mathbf{j}$, $t = 3$ f $\mathbf{u} = 3\mathbf{i} - 4\mathbf{j}$, $\mathbf{v} = 5\mathbf{i} + 12\mathbf{j}$, $t = 4$

10   A particle P is accelerating at 2.6 ms^{-2} from A to B. The velocity of P at A is $(2\mathbf{i} - 3\mathbf{j})$ ms^{-1} and at B is $(7\mathbf{i} + 9\mathbf{j})$ ms^{-1}.

Find the acceleration in the form $(\lambda\mathbf{i} + \mu\mathbf{j})$.

11   A particle has initial velocity $\mathbf{u}$ ms^{-1}. The particle moves with uniform acceleration $\mathbf{a}$ ms^{-2} and after t seconds it has velocity $\mathbf{v}$ ms^{-1}.

Find $\mathbf{v}$ when

a $\mathbf{u} = 3\mathbf{i}$, $\mathbf{a} = \mathbf{i}$, $t = 2$ b $\mathbf{u} = 2\mathbf{i}$, $\mathbf{a} = 2\mathbf{j}$, $t = 3$

c $\mathbf{u} = \mathbf{i} + \mathbf{j}$, $\mathbf{a} = -2\mathbf{j}$, $t = 4$ d $\mathbf{u} = 2\mathbf{i} + \mathbf{j}$, $\mathbf{a} = \mathbf{i} + 5\mathbf{j}$, $t = 2$

e $\mathbf{u} = 4\mathbf{i} - \mathbf{j}$, $\mathbf{a} = -\mathbf{i} + \mathbf{j}$, $t = 5$ f $\mathbf{u} = \frac{3}{2}\mathbf{i} - 2\mathbf{j}$, $\mathbf{a} = 2\mathbf{i} + \frac{1}{2}\mathbf{j}$, $t = 3$

12   At time $t = 0$ a particle is moving with velocity $(\mathbf{i} + 3\mathbf{j})$ ms^{-1}. It is subject to a constant acceleration for 4 seconds until it reaches a velocity $(6\mathbf{i} - 9\mathbf{j})$ ms^{-1}.

Find the magnitude of the acceleration and the angle it makes with the vector $\mathbf{j}$ correct to the nearest degree.

13   A particle has initial velocity $(-2\mathbf{i} + \mathbf{j})$ ms^{-1} and accelerates in the direction $(3\mathbf{i} - 4\mathbf{j})$. The magnitude of the acceleration is 2.5 ms^{-2}.

Find to 3 sf the speed of the particle after 6 seconds.

14   At time $t = 0$ a particle at the origin O begins moving with uniform velocity $(2\mathbf{i} + 3\mathbf{j})$ ms^{-1} where $\mathbf{i}$ and $\mathbf{j}$ are unit vectors due east and north respectively.

a   Find an expression for the position vector of the particle at time t seconds.

b   Find the time at which the particle is due north of the point with position vector $(4\mathbf{i} + \mathbf{j})$ m.

15 A particle P is at the point with position vector $3\mathbf{i}$ m. At time $t = 0$, P begins to move with uniform velocity $(\mathbf{i} + 2\mathbf{j})$ ms^{-1} where $\mathbf{i}$ and $\mathbf{j}$ are unit vectors due east and north respectively.

    a Find an expression for the position vector of P at time t seconds.

    The point A has position vector $2\mathbf{j}$ m.

    b Find the displacement vector $\overrightarrow{AP}$ in terms of t.

    c Find the position vector of P when it is north-east of A.

16 Initially particle P is at the point with position vector $(\mathbf{i} - \mathbf{j})$ m. At time $t = 0$, P begins moving with uniform velocity $(\mathbf{i} + \mathbf{j})$ ms^{-1}.

    a Find an expression for the position vector of P at time t seconds.

    b Show that the distance, d metres, of P from the point with position vector $(7\mathbf{i} + \mathbf{j})$ m is given by $d^2 = 2(t^2 - 8t + 20)$.

    c By expressing d^2 in the form $a(t + b)^2 + c$, or otherwise, find the value of t for which d^2 is a minimum and hence find the least distance of P from the point with position vector $(7\mathbf{i} + \mathbf{j})$ m correct to 2 significant figures.

17 At time $t = 0$, particle P is at the point with position vector $6\mathbf{j}$ m and particle Q is at the point with position vector $3\mathbf{i}$ m. P and Q move with constant velocities $(3\mathbf{i} - 4\mathbf{j})$ ms^{-1} and $(2\mathbf{i} - 2\mathbf{j})$ ms^{-1} respectively.

    a Find the position vector of P at time t seconds.

    b Find the position vector of Q at time t seconds.

    c Find the value of t when P and Q collide and their position vector at this time.

18 At time $t = 0$, particle A is at the origin O and moving with constant velocity $(2\mathbf{i} + \mathbf{j})$ ms^{-1}. At the same instant particle B is at the point with position vector $(-4\mathbf{i} + 20\mathbf{j})$ m and moving with constant velocity $(3\mathbf{i} - 4\mathbf{j})$ ms^{-1}.

    a Find the position vectors of A and B after t seconds.

    b Show that, if they maintain their current paths, A and B will collide. Find the time when this will occur.

    However, when $t = 2$ seconds particle A changes direction and moves with constant velocity $2\mathbf{i}$ ms^{-1}.

    c Find the distance between A and B when $t = 4$.

19 At time $t = 0$ particle A is at the point with position vector $4\mathbf{i}$ m and particle B is at the point with position vector $3\mathbf{j}$ m where $\mathbf{i}$ and $\mathbf{j}$ are unit vectors due east and north respectively. A and B are moving with constant velocities $(\mathbf{i} + 2\mathbf{j})$ ms^{-1} and $(2\mathbf{i} + \mathbf{j})$ ms^{-1} respectively.

    a Show that at time t seconds $\overrightarrow{AB} = [(t - 4)\mathbf{i} + (3 - t)\mathbf{j}]$ m.

    b Find the time at which B is due west of A.

    c Find the time at which A and B are closest.

Exercise 6E   Exam Practice

1   A particle initially travels with velocity $(i - 7j)$ ms^{-1}, where i and j are perpendicular unit vectors. The particle accelerates uniformly and 10 seconds later is travelling in the same direction with velocity $(5i + aj)$ ms^{-1}.

   a   State the value of a.   **(1 mark)**

   b   Find the acceleration of the particle in vector form.   **(3 marks)**

   c   Find to the nearest degree the angle that the acceleration of the particle makes with the vector i.   **(2 marks)**

2   A ship sets sail at 8 a.m. from a port and moves with uniform velocity. Relative to a fixed origin, O, the position vector of the port is $(5i - 16j)$ km where i and j are unit vectors directed due east and north respectively. At 8.24 a.m. the ship is at the point with position vector $(3i - 12j)$ km.

   a   Find the velocity of the ship.   **(3 marks)**

   b   Find the position vector of the ship at h hours after 8 a.m.   **(2 marks)**

   At 9 a.m. a passenger on the ship notices that *Gannet Island* is due north of the ship. At 10 a.m. the passenger sees that the island is now north-east of the ship.

   c   Find the position vector of *Gannet Island*.   **(6 marks)**

   d   Find the time at which *Gannet Island* will be due east of the ship.   **(3 marks)**

3   A car is travelling with constant velocity $(15i + \beta j)$ ms^{-1} where $\beta < 0$ and i and j are perpendicular unit vectors. The current speed of the car is 17 ms^{-1}, but a speed limit restriction ahead requires the car to decrease its speed to 13 ms^{-1} whilst continuing in the same direction.

   Find the new velocity of the car.   **(4 marks)**

4   Alex and Sally are members of a microlite club. During one flight, Alex is 200 m south of the base O at 2:30 p.m. travelling at $(8i + 20j)$ ms^{-1}, where i and j are unit vectors due east and north respectively. At this time Sally is 300 m west and 150 m south of Alex travelling at $(10i + 22j)$ ms^{-1} at the same altitude.

   a   Find the position vectors of Alex and Sally relative to O at time t seconds after 2:30 p.m.   **(3 marks)**

   b   Given that Alex and Sally continue with constant velocity, find to the nearest metre the minimum distance between them, and the exact time at which they are closest.   **(8 marks)**

5   Two lambs, Andrew and Bryony, are playing in a field. At time $t = 0$,
     Andrew is at a fixed point O in the field and Bryony is at the point
     with position vector $(-3\mathbf{i} + 6\mathbf{j})$ m relative to O, where $\mathbf{i}$ and $\mathbf{j}$ are
     perpendicular unit vectors in the plane of the field.

     Andrew is moving with constant velocity towards the point with
     position vector $(6\mathbf{i} + 8\mathbf{j})$ m. Bryony is moving with constant velocity
     towards the point with position vector $15\mathbf{i}$ m. Given that Andrew's
     speed is 1.25 ms^{-1} and Bryony's speed is $\sqrt{10}$ ms^{-1},

     a   find, in vector form, Andrew's velocity,   **(3 marks)**

     b   show that Bryony has velocity $(3\mathbf{i} - \mathbf{j})$ ms^{-1}.   **(4 marks)**

     At time $t = 2$ seconds, Bryony is at the point P.

     c   Show that Andrew also passes through the point P.   **(4 marks)**

     d   Find to 2 significant figures how far apart the lambs are when
         Andrew is at the point P.   **(4 marks)**

6   Relative to a fixed origin O a particle P has position vector

     $$\mathbf{r}_P = [(t^2 + 1)\mathbf{i} + (9t - 6)\mathbf{j}] \text{ m}$$

     at time t seconds where $\mathbf{i}$ and $\mathbf{j}$ are perpendicular unit vectors.

     a   Find the values of t when $\mathbf{r}_P$ is parallel to the vector $(2\mathbf{i} + 3\mathbf{j})$.   **(4 marks)**

     The position vector of particle Q at time t seconds is

     $$\mathbf{r}_Q = [(t^2 + 1)\mathbf{i} + 6t\mathbf{j}] \text{ m}.$$

     b   Find the positive value of t when the magnitude of $\mathbf{r}_Q$ is 13 m and
         find the distance between P and Q at this time.   **(6 marks)**

7   At 1 p.m. Liz is sat on a bench, O, in a park and her friend Jackie is at
     the point with position vector $(-384\mathbf{i} + 348\mathbf{j})$ m relative to O where
     $\mathbf{i}$ and $\mathbf{j}$ are unit vectors due east and due north respectively.

     Jackie immediately starts walking with constant velocity. Liz leaves
     the bench 2 minutes later and walks with constant velocity. The
     position vectors of Liz and Jackie at time $t = 130$ seconds after 1 p.m.
     are $\mathbf{r}_L = (-12\mathbf{i} + 9\mathbf{j})$ m and $\mathbf{r}_J = (-254\mathbf{i} + 218\mathbf{j})$ m respectively.

     a   Show that Liz walks with speed 1.5 ms^{-1}.   **(3 marks)**

     b   Find the position vector of Jackie at time t seconds after 1 p.m.   **(4 marks)**

     c   Show that the displacement vector of Liz from Jackie at time
         t seconds after 1 p.m. for $t \geq 120$ is

         $$[(2.2t - 528)\mathbf{i} + (456 - 1.9t)\mathbf{j}] \text{ m}.$$ **(4 marks)**

     d   Show that Liz and Jackie will meet if they continue walking with
         the same velocities and find the exact time at which this happens. **(3 marks)**

8   Particle P is moving with constant velocity $(-2\mathbf{i} + \mathbf{j})\ \mathrm{ms}^{-1}$ where $\mathbf{i}$ and $\mathbf{j}$ are unit vectors directed due east and north respectively. At time $t = 0$, P passes through the point with position vector $(14\mathbf{i} + 2\mathbf{j})$ m relative to a fixed origin O.

    a   Find the position vector of P at time t seconds.   **(2 marks)**

    b   Find the time at which P is north-east of O.   **(3 marks)**

    c   Show that P is at a distance of 9 m or less from O for 3.6 seconds. **(7 marks)**

9   At 12 noon, two ships A and B are located such that A has position vector $(24\mathbf{i} - 29\mathbf{j})$ km and B has position vector $3\mathbf{j}$ km relative to a fixed origin O, where $\mathbf{i}$ and $\mathbf{j}$ are unit vectors due east and north respectively. A is travelling with velocity $(2\mathbf{i} + 13\mathbf{j})\ \mathrm{kmh}^{-1}$ and B is travelling with velocity $(6\mathbf{i} + 9\mathbf{j})\ \mathrm{kmh}^{-1}$.

    a   Find the position vector of A at time h hours after 12 noon.   **(2 marks)**

    b   Find the vector $\overrightarrow{AB}$ at time h hours after 12 noon.   **(3 marks)**

    c   Show that the distance, d km, between the ships at time h hours after 12 noon satisfies $d^2 = 32(h^2 - 14h + 50)$.   **(4 marks)**

    d   Calculate to 2 significant figures the closest distance between the two ships during their journeys if each maintains the same course. **(4 marks)**

10   Relative to a fixed origin O, a car travels from the point with position vector $(45\mathbf{i} - 117\mathbf{j})$ m, where $\mathbf{i}$ and $\mathbf{j}$ are unit vectors due east and north respectively, to the point with position vector $(-98\mathbf{i} + 130\mathbf{j})$ m in 13 seconds at constant velocity.

    a   Calculate the velocity of the car and hence show that the speed of the car is $22.0\ \mathrm{ms}^{-1}$, correct to 3 significant figures.   **(4 marks)**

    b   Calculate the acute angle between the direction of motion of the car and the vector $\mathbf{j}$, giving your answer to the nearest degree. **(2 marks)**

11   Two spheres P and Q both have a radius of 4 cm. At time $t = 0$, the centre of P has position vector $\mathbf{r}_P = (-38\mathbf{i} - 2\mathbf{j})$ cm, relative to a fixed origin O, and the centre of Q has position vector $\mathbf{r}_Q = (-3\mathbf{i} + 16\mathbf{j})$ cm, where $\mathbf{i}$ and $\mathbf{j}$ are perpendicular unit vectors. The spheres are moving with constant velocities $\mathbf{v}_P = (8\mathbf{i} - \mathbf{j})\ \mathrm{cms}^{-1}$ and $\mathbf{v}_Q = (5\mathbf{i} - 3\mathbf{j})\ \mathrm{cms}^{-1}$ respectively.

    a   Find the position vector of the centre of P at time t seconds.   **(2 marks)**

    b   Find an expression for d^2 in terms of t, where d cm is the distance between the centres of the two spheres.   **(6 marks)**

    c   Find the value of t when the spheres collide.   **(4 marks)**

Resolving and Resultant Forces

Exercise 7S   Skills Practice

In questions 1 and 2 give the magnitude of the resultant force correct to 3 sf where appropriate and give its direction as a bearing to the nearest degree, taking due north as vertically up the page.

1   Find the magnitude and direction of the resultant force in each case.

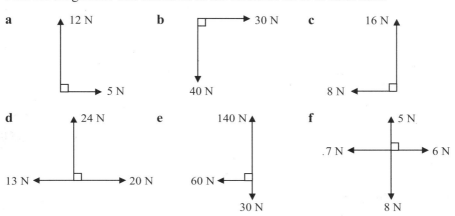

2   Find the magnitude and bearing of the resultant force in each case.

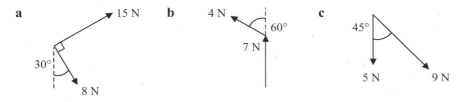

In questions 3 to 9, **i** and **j** are perpendicular unit vectors.

3   Find in vector form the resultant of the forces $\mathbf{F}_1$, $\mathbf{F}_2$ and $\mathbf{F}_3$ given that

    a $\mathbf{F}_1 = (\mathbf{i} - 8\mathbf{j})$ N, $\mathbf{F}_2 = (3\mathbf{i} + 2\mathbf{j})$ N and $\mathbf{F}_3 = (-7\mathbf{i} - 4\mathbf{j})$ N,

    b $\mathbf{F}_1 = (4\mathbf{i} - \mathbf{j})$ N, $\mathbf{F}_2 = (-5\mathbf{i} + 2\mathbf{j})$ N and $\mathbf{F}_3 = (\mathbf{i} - \mathbf{j})$ N,

    c $\mathbf{F}_1 = (2\mathbf{i} + \frac{1}{2}\mathbf{j})$ N, $\mathbf{F}_2 = (\frac{5}{2}\mathbf{i} - 3\mathbf{j})$ N and $\mathbf{F}_3 = (-\mathbf{i} + \frac{7}{4}\mathbf{j})$ N.

4   The resultant of the forces $\mathbf{F}_1$, $\mathbf{F}_2$ and $\mathbf{F}_3$ is denoted by $\mathbf{F}$. Find λ and μ given that

    a $\mathbf{F}_1 = (2\mathbf{i} + \lambda\mathbf{j})$ N, $\mathbf{F}_2 = (3\mathbf{i} - 2\mathbf{j})$ N, $\mathbf{F}_3 = (\mu\mathbf{i} + \mathbf{j})$ N and $\mathbf{F} = 6\mathbf{i}$ N,

    b $\mathbf{F}_1 = \lambda\mathbf{i}$ N, $\mathbf{F}_2 = (2\lambda\mathbf{i} - \mu\mathbf{j})$ N, $\mathbf{F}_3 = (\lambda\mathbf{i} + 2\mu\mathbf{j})$ N and $\mathbf{F} = 8\mathbf{i} - 3\mathbf{j}$ N,

    c $\mathbf{F}_1 = (3\lambda\mathbf{i} + 2\lambda\mathbf{j})$ N, $\mathbf{F}_2 = (2\mathbf{i} - \mu\mathbf{j})$ N, $\mathbf{F}_3 = (2\mu\mathbf{i} + \mathbf{j})$ N and $\mathbf{F} = 6\mathbf{i} + 6\mathbf{j}$ N.

5   Two forces $(8\mathbf{i} - 2\mathbf{j})$ N and $(-3\mathbf{i} + k\mathbf{j})$ N act on a particle.

Given that the resultant force acting on the particle is parallel to the vector $(\mathbf{i} - 2\mathbf{j})$ find the value of k.

6   Find the magnitude of the force $\mathbf{F}$ where $\mathbf{F} = (14\mathbf{i} + 48\mathbf{j})$ N.

Find also the acute angle that $\mathbf{F}$ makes with the vector $\mathbf{i}$ in degrees to 1 dp.

7   Three forces $(2\mathbf{i} + 3\mathbf{j})$ N, $(3\mathbf{i} - 5\mathbf{j})$ N and $4\mathbf{i}$ N act on a particle.

a   Find the resultant force acting on the particle in the form $(a\mathbf{i} + b\mathbf{j})$ N.

b   Find to 2 sf the magnitude of the resultant force acting on the particle.

c   Find to the nearest degree the angle the resultant force makes with the vector $\mathbf{i}$.

8   The resultant of the forces $(4\mathbf{i} + 15\mathbf{j})$ N and $(a\mathbf{i} + 9\mathbf{j})$ N has magnitude 25 N.

Given that $a > 0$, find the value of a.

9   A body is acted upon by forces of $(\lambda\mathbf{i} - 5\mathbf{j})$ N, $(-\mathbf{i} + 2\lambda\mathbf{j})$ N and $(4\mathbf{i} - 9\mathbf{j})$ N.

Given that the resultant force acting on the body has magnitude 10 N, find the possible values of λ.

10   Resolve each force in the directions of the positive x and y-axes.
Give your answers as the product of the force and a trigonometric ratio.

a 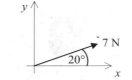   **b** 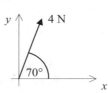   **c**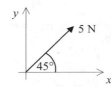

d 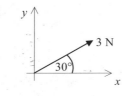   **e** 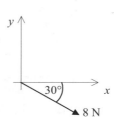   **f**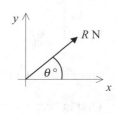

11   In each case express the component of the given force in the direction $\overrightarrow{AB}$.
Give your answers as the product of the force and a trigonometric ratio.

a 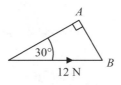   **b** 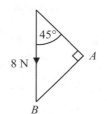   **c**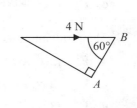

12 Find the magnitude of the components of each force parallel and perpendicular to the inclined plane, giving your answers correct to 3 sf where appropriate.

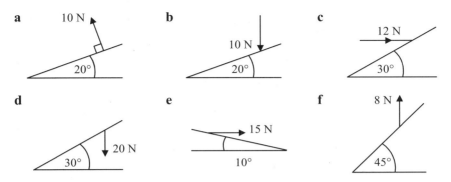

13 The forces shown act on a particle at the origin O. Find the magnitude of the resultant force acting on the particle and the angle it makes with the positive x-axis, giving your answers to 3 sf.

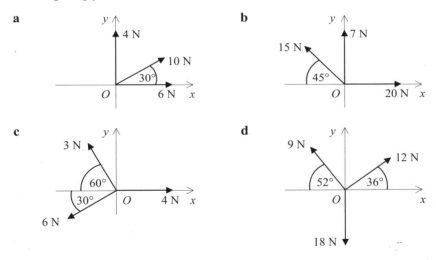

14 A particle P is subject to a 10 N force acting due north, a 20 N force acting due west and a force of magnitude A N acting on a bearing of 120°.

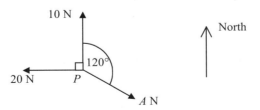

Given that the resultant force on the particle acts on a bearing of 225°, find the value of A correct to 3 significant figures.

Equilibrium

1   A particle is held in equilibrium by the forces shown.

Find in exact form the magnitude of forces P and Q in each case.

a
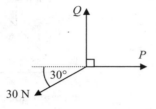

b
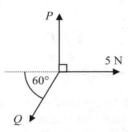

c
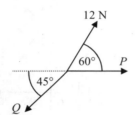

d
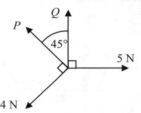

2   A particle is held in equilibrium by the forces shown. Find, correct to 3 sf where appropriate, the magnitude of force P and the size of angle θ in degrees.

a
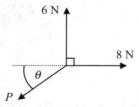

b
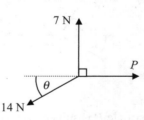

c
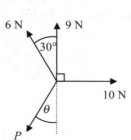

d
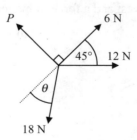

In questions 3 to 6, **i** and **j** are perpendicular unit vectors.

3   A particle is in equilibrium under the action of three forces $(3\mathbf{i} - 2\mathbf{j})$ N, $(-5\mathbf{i} + \mathbf{j})$ N and $(\lambda\mathbf{i} + \mu\mathbf{j})$ N. Find λ and μ.

4   A particle is in equilibrium under the action of the forces $(3\lambda\mathbf{i} - \mu\mathbf{j})$ N, $(2\mu\mathbf{i} + 8\mathbf{j})$ N and $(5\mathbf{i} + 2\lambda\mathbf{j})$ N. Find λ and μ.

5   Three forces $\mathbf{F}_1$, $\mathbf{F}_2$ and $\mathbf{F}_3$ act on a particle P. Given that $\mathbf{F}_1 = (3\mathbf{i} - 7\mathbf{j})$ N, $\mathbf{F}_2 = (-8\mathbf{i} + 3\mathbf{j})$ N and that P is in equilibrium, find the magnitude of $\mathbf{F}_3$ correct to 2 sf and the angle it makes with the vector **i** to the nearest degree.

6   Three forces $\mathbf{F}_1$, $\mathbf{F}_2$ and $\mathbf{F}_3$ act on a particle P. Given that $\mathbf{F}_1 = (t^2\mathbf{i} - 5\mathbf{j})$ N, $\mathbf{F}_2 = (t\mathbf{i} + 3\mathbf{j})$ N and $\mathbf{F}_3 = (-6\mathbf{i} + 2\mathbf{j})$ N and that P is in equilibrium, find the two possible values of t.

7   A book of mass 2 kg is at rest on a horizontal table.

    a Draw a diagram showing all the forces acting on the book.

    b Write down in terms of g the magnitude of each of the forces in your diagram.

8   A ball of mass 400 g is suspended by a string and hangs in equilibrium.

    a Draw a diagram showing all the forces acting on the ball.

    b Write down in terms of g the magnitude of each of the forces in your diagram.

9   A particle of weight 40 N is suspended from a light inextensible string. The particle is acted upon by a horizontal force, H, so that when the particle is in equilibrium it makes an angle of 30° with the vertical as shown below.

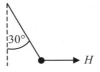

    a Draw a diagram showing all the forces acting on the particle.

    b Find the tension in the string correct to 3 sf.

    c Find H correct to 3 sf.

10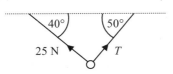

A particle is suspended by two light inextensible strings and hangs in equilibrium. The strings are inclined at 40° and 50° to the horizontal and have tensions of 25 N and T N respectively.

    a Find T correct to 3 sf.

    b Find the mass of the particle correct to 2 sf.

11 A jacket on a coathanger is suspended in equilibrium by two light inextensible strings each inclined at an angle θ to the horizontal. The combined mass of the jacket and coathanger is 0.8 kg.

    a Find to 2 sf the tension in the strings when $\theta = 30°$.

    Given that the strings will break under tension of more than 10 N,

    b find, to the nearest degree, the minimum value of θ for which the strings do not break.

12 A block is at rest in equilibrium on a smooth plane. Find in each case the magnitude of the force F and the normal reaction R, giving your answers to an appropriate degree of accuracy.

    a

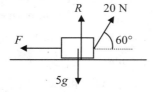

    b

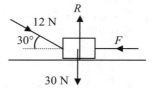

13 A particle of weight 20 N is at rest in equilibrium on a smooth inclined plane under the action of a force P. In each case draw the forces acting on the particle and find the magnitude of P.

    a

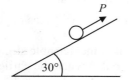

    b

14 A particle of mass 2 kg is held at rest in equilibrium on a smooth plane inclined at an angle of 25° to the horizontal by a force of magnitude F N.

    Find to 2 sf the value of F if it is directed

    a parallel to the plane,

    b horizontally.

15

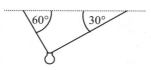

    A lamp of mass 1.5 kg is suspended from the roof of a tent by two light inextensible strings which are inclined at 30° and 60° to the horizontal.

    Given that the light is in equilibrium, find the tension in each string correct to 2 sf.

Exercise 8E   Exam Practice

1   A particle is in equilibrium when subjected to forces $\mathbf{F}_1$, $\mathbf{F}_2$ and $\mathbf{F}_3$.

Given that $\mathbf{F}_1 = (3\mathbf{i} + 11\mathbf{j})$ N and $\mathbf{F}_2 = (9\mathbf{i} - 2\mathbf{j})$ N, where $\mathbf{i}$ and $\mathbf{j}$ are perpendicular unit vectors, find the magnitude of $\mathbf{F}_3$ and the angle it makes with the vector $\mathbf{j}$ correct to the nearest degree.   **(6 marks)**

2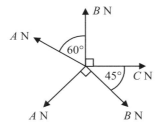

A particle remains in equilibrium when subjected to two forces of magnitude A N, two forces of magnitude B N and one force of magnitude C N, directed as shown in the diagram above.

Show that $A : B = \sqrt{2} : 1$.   **(7 marks)**

3

A particle of weight 60 N is held in equilibrium under gravity by two forces of magnitude X N and Y N. The force of X N is horizontal and the force of Y N is directed upwards at 25° to the horizontal. Both forces are in the same vertical plane.

Find the values of X and Y correct to 3 significant figures.   **(5 marks)**

4   A particle P, of mass 20 kg, is at rest on a smooth horizontal plane and is attached to a vertical post on the plane by a light inextensible string. The string can withstand tension of up to 130 N before breaking. The plane is then inclined with the string taut and parallel to the plane and the post higher up the plane than P.

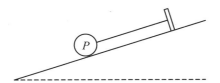

Find the angle of inclination of the plane at which the string will break, giving your answer to the nearest degree.   **(4 marks)**

5   A cable car of weight 5500 N is at rest in equilibrium hanging from
     a point on a cable. The cable makes an angle of 5° with the horizontal
     on one side of the car and 3° on the other side.

     Find the tension in the cable on either side of the car, giving your
     answers correct to 3 significant figues.   **(7 marks)**

6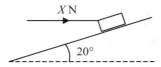

     A block of mass 15 kg is held at rest on a smooth plane inclined at
     20° to the horizontal by a force of magnitude X N directed
     horizontally towards the plane. The force is in a vertical plane
     containing a line of greatest slope of the plane.

     Find the value of X correct to an appropriate degree of accuracy.   **(4 marks)**

7   A particle is in equilibrium when subjected to forces $\mathbf{F}_1$, $\mathbf{F}_2$ and $\mathbf{F}_3$.
     The force $\mathbf{F}_1 = (3\mathbf{i} - \mathbf{j})$ N where $\mathbf{i}$ and $\mathbf{j}$ are perpendicular unit vectors.

     Given that $\mathbf{F}_2$ is parallel to the vector $(\mathbf{i} - 2\mathbf{j})$ and $\mathbf{F}_3$ is parallel to the
     vector $(-2\mathbf{i} + 3\mathbf{j})$ find $\mathbf{F}_2$ and $\mathbf{F}_3$.   **(6 marks)**

8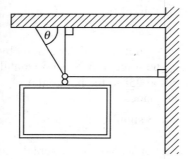

     A shop sign of mass 20 kg is suspended by two strings from an
     overhanging horizontal beam, one of which is vertical while the
     other is inclined at an angle θ to the horizontal. The sign is kept in
     equilibrium by a horizontal string attached to a wall and all three
     strings are in the same vertical plane. The tension in the horizontal
     string is half the tension in the angled string. The tension in the
     vertical string is three times the tension in the angled string.

     a   Find θ in degrees.   **(3 marks)**

     b   Find to 2 significant figures the tension in the vertical string.   **(5 marks)**

Friction

1　Draw a diagram to show all the forces acting on

　a　a particle at rest on a rough horizontal plane subject to a horizontal force P,

　b　a particle at rest on a rough inclined plane subject to a force Q acting parallel to the plane such that the particle is on the point of moving up the plane,

　c　a particle at rest on a rough inclined plane subject to a horizontal force F directed towards the plane such that the particle is on the point of moving down the plane.

2

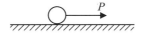

A particle of mass 2 kg is at rest on a rough horizontal plane and is being acted upon by a horizontal force P.

　a　Find the normal reaction exerted on the particle by the plane in terms of g.

Given that the particle is in limiting equilibrium and that the coefficient of friction between the particle and the plane is 0.6,

　b　find P correct to 2 sf.

3　A box of weight 25 N remains at rest on a rough horizontal plane when it is subjected to a horizontal force of 20 N. Given that the box is on the point of moving, find the coefficient of friction between the box and the plane.

4　A block at rest on a rough plane is subjected to a horizontal force. The coefficient of friction between the block and the plane is μ. Find whether or not the block will move and if it remains at rest, find if it is in limiting equilibrium.

a
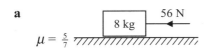

b
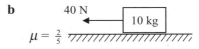

c
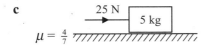

d

5　In each part of this question a block is in limiting equilibrium on a rough horizontal plane. Find the force P in terms of g in each case.

a　　　　　　　　　　　　　　　　　**b**
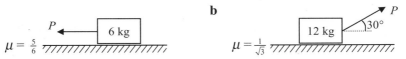

6

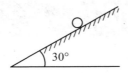

A particle of weight 8 N is at rest in limiting equilibrium on a rough plane inclined at an angle of 30° to the horizontal. Find in exact form

a the normal reaction exerted by the plane on the block,

b the frictional force acting on the particle,

c the coefficient of friction between the particle and the plane.

7 A box of mass 4 kg is placed on a rough plane inclined at an angle θ to the horizontal. The coefficient of friction between the box and the plane is $\frac{1}{2}$.

Find to the nearest degree the maximum value of θ for which the box will remain at rest.

8

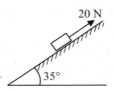

A particle of mass 5 kg is at rest on a rough plane inclined at an angle of 35° to the horizontal. When the particle is held by a force of 20 N acting parallel to the slope it is on the point of slipping down the plane.

Find to 2 sf the coefficient of friction between the particle and the plane.

9

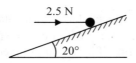

A particle of mass 3 kg is held on the point of sliding down a rough plane inclined at an angle of 20° to the horizontal by a horizontal force of 2.5 N.

Find to 2 sf the coefficient of friction between the particle and the plane.

10 A particle of weight 30 N is held at rest on a rough plane inclined at an angle of 45° to the horizontal by a force of magnitude H N acting parallel to and up the slope. The coefficient of friction between the particle and the plane is $\frac{1}{3}$.

Find in exact form

a the minimum value of H required to prevent the particle slipping down the plane,

b the maximum value of H for which the particle does not slip up the plane.

Exercise 9E   Exam Practice

1   A particle of mass 10 kg is at rest on a rough plane inclined at an angle θ to the horizontal. The coefficient of friction between the particle and the plane is $\frac{3}{4}$.

Given that the particle is on the point of slipping find the exact value of cos θ.   **(6 marks)**

2

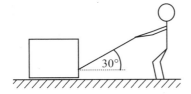

Sanjay is attempting to pull a large box of goods of total mass 40 kg along a rough horizontal floor using a light inextensible string. When the string makes an angle of 30° with the horizontal and the tension in the string is 150 N the box does not move.

By modelling the box as a particle, find to an appropriate degree of accuracy the minimum value of the coefficient of friction between the box and the floor.   **(6 marks)**

3   A container P, of weight 5 kN, is at rest on a rough horizontal pláne. When a horizontal force of 1 kN is applied to P it is in limiting equilibrium.

P is then attached to a light inextensible string, the other end of which is fixed at the point A on the plane. With the string taut the plane is tilted so that AP is parallel to a line of greatest slope of the plane with A higher than P. Given that the maximum angle at which the plane may be inclined to the horizontal without the string breaking is 25°, find to 2 significant figures the maximum tension which the string can withstand.   **(9 marks)**

4

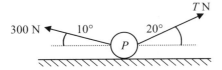

A parcel P, of mass 50 kg, is at rest on a rough horizontal plane. The coefficient of friction between P and the plane is 0.4

P is subjected to forces of 300 N and T N in the same vertical plane which make angles of 10° and 20° respectively with the horizontal as shown. Find correct to 2 significant figures the minimum value of T for which P remains in equilibrium.   **(8 marks)**

5   Scott and his son Harry are attempting to pull a block of mass 100 kg along rough horizontal ground using ropes. They are, however, pulling in opposite directions with horizontal forces of 300 N and 50 N respectively.

Given that the box is on the point of sliding, find to 2 significant figures the coefficient of friction between the box and the ground.   **(5 marks)**

6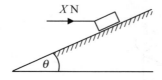

A body of mass m kg is at rest on a rough plane inclined at an angle θ to the horizontal. It is on the point of sliding down the plane, held by a horizontal force of X N in the same vertical plane as a line of greatest slope of the plane. The coefficient of friction between the body and the plane is μ.

Show that $X = \dfrac{mg(\tan \theta - \mu)}{1 + \mu \tan \theta}$.   **(8 marks)**

7   A particle is at rest on a rough horizontal plane. The plane is then tilted until, when it is inclined at an angle θ to the horizontal, the particle is on the point of sliding.

Prove that the coefficient of friction between the particle and the plane is tan θ.   **(6 marks)**

8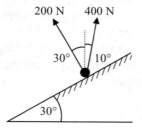

A parcel of mass 90 kg is at rest on a rough plane inclined at an angle of 30° to the horizontal, supported by two light inextensible strings. The strings make angles of 10° and 30° with the vertical and the tensions in the strings are 400 N and 200 N respectively.

Given that the particle is on the point of sliding down the plane, find the coefficient of friction between the particle and the plane correct to 2 significant figures.   **(8 marks)**

Statics Review

Exercise 10E   Exam Practice

1   A body is acted upon by the forces $(16\mathbf{i} + 3\mathbf{j})$ N, $(4\mathbf{i} - 5\mathbf{j})$ N and
$(a\mathbf{i} + 8\mathbf{j})$ N where $\mathbf{i}$ and $\mathbf{j}$ are perpendicular unit vectors. Given that
the resultant force is parallel to the vector $(3\mathbf{i} + \mathbf{j})$ find the value of a.   **(4 marks)**

2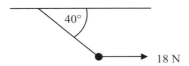

A particle hangs from a light inextensible string the other end of
which is attached to a horizontal plane. When a horizontal force
of 18 N acts on the particle it rests in equilibrium with the string
making an angle of 40° with the plane.

   a   Find the tension in the string correct to 3 significant figures.   **(3 marks)**

   b   Find the weight of the particle correct to 3 significant figures.   **(3 marks)**

3   A particle P of mass 20 kg is placed on a smooth plane inclined at an
angle θ to the horizontal where $\cos\theta = \frac{24}{25}$. P is held at rest by a
force of X N acting parallel to a line of greatest slope of the plane.

Find in terms of g

   a   the magnitude of the normal reaction exerted by the plane on P,   **(3 marks)**

   b   the value of X.   **(3 marks)**

4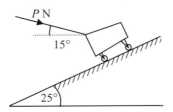

A man of mass 70 kg is standing on a rough plane inclined at an angle
of 25° to the horizontal. He is holding a shopping trolley and its
contents, of total mass 35 kg, at rest higher up the plane by applying a
force P N to the trolley. The force acts at an angle of 15° to the
horizontal and in the same vertical plane as a line of greatest slope of
the plane as shown. The coefficient of friction between the trolley
and the plane is 0.4

By modelling the trolley and its contents as a particle, find the
maximum value of P correct to 2 significant figures.   **(8 marks)**

5

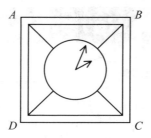

A circular clock of mass 5 kg is suspended in the centre of a square frame by four wires. The wires are of equal length and joined to the corners of the frame A, B, C and D such that each makes an angle of 45° with the horizontal.

Given that the lower wires, joined to C and D, are subject to 25% of the tension in the upper wires, joined to A and B, find the exact magnitude of the tension in the upper wires in terms of g.   **(6 marks)**

6

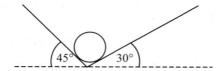

A sphere of mass 500 g is at rest against two smooth planes inclined at angles of 45° and 30° to the horizontal. The centre of the sphere is in a vertical plane containing a line of greatest slope of each of the inclined planes.

Find in terms of g the exact magnitude of the normal reaction exerted on the sphere by each plane.   **(9 marks)**

7   A particle P of mass m kg is at rest on a rough horizontal plane. Horizontal forces of magnitude X N and $2X$ N act on P in opposite directions and P is kept in equilibrium. Given that the coefficient of friction between P and the plane is μ, find an expression for the minimum value of μ in terms of m, X and g.   **(4 marks)**

8

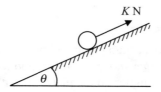

K N

A particle of mass m kg is held at rest on a rough plane inclined at an angle θ to the horizontal by a force of magnitude K N acting parallel to a line of greatest slope of the plane. Given that the coefficient of friction between the particle and the plane is μ, show that the minimum value of K is $mg(\sin \theta - \mu \cos \theta)$.   **(6 marks)**

9   The force $[(2p + 3)\mathbf{i} + (4p - 7)\mathbf{j}]$ N, where $\mathbf{i}$ and $\mathbf{j}$ are perpendicular unit vectors, has magnitude $\sqrt{37}$ N.

Find the possible values of the constant p.   **(6 marks)**

10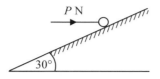

A rough plane is inclined at an angle of 30° to the horizontal. A particle of mass m kg is at rest in equilibrium on the plane under the application of a horizontal force P N directed towards the plane and in the same vertical plane as a line of greatest slope of the plane. The coefficient of friction between the particle and the plane is μ.

Show that $\dfrac{mg(1 - \mu\sqrt{3})}{\sqrt{3} + \mu} \leq P \leq \dfrac{mg(1 + \mu\sqrt{3})}{\sqrt{3} - \mu}$.   **(12 marks)**

11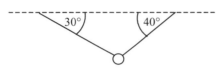

A particle of mass 400 g is attached to a point on a light inextensible string. When the particle is at rest in equilibrium the sections of string on either side of the particle make angles of 30° and 40° with the horizontal.

Find to an appropriate degree of accuracy the tension in each section of string.   **(8 marks)**

12

A sphere of weight 98 N is at rest hanging from a vertical light inextensible string. The sphere is pushed against a rough wall by a force of magnitude 40 N acting at an angle of 30° to the horizontal as shown. The coefficient of friction between the sphere and the wall is $\frac{1}{2}$. Find in the form $m + n\sqrt{3}$ the minimum tension in the string for which the sphere is in equilibrium.   **(7 marks)**

Motion - Newton's Laws

Exercise 11S   Skills Practice

1   A particle of mass 2 kg is accelerating at 3 ms^{-2}.

Find the magnitude of the resultant force acting on the particle.

2   Find the acceleration of a particle of mass 500 g being acted on by a resultant force of magnitude 9 N.

3   A particle accelerates at 2 ms^{-2} when subjected to a resultant force of magnitude 10 N. Find the mass of the particle.

4   Find the acceleration of a particle of mass 2.5 kg when subjected to a resultant force of magnitude 18 N.

5   At time $t = 0$, a resultant force of magnitude 24 N is applied to a particle of mass 6 kg which is at rest.

    a   Find the acceleration of the particle.

    b · Find the speed of the particle when $t = 3$ seconds.

6   A particle of mass 3 kg is moving with speed 18 ms^{-1}. A resultant force of magnitude 12 N acting in the opposite direction to the particle's motion is used to bring the particle to rest.

    a   Find the magnitude of the particle's deceleration.

    b   Find the distance travelled by the particle during this deceleration.

7   A particle of mass 600 g is moving along a straight line at 3 ms^{-1}. The speed of the particle is increased to 12 ms^{-1} by the action of a constant resultant force of magnitude 4 N. Find the length of time for which the force acts on the particle.

8   In each case the forces acting on a particle of mass 5 kg are shown. Find, correct to 3 sf where appropriate, the magnitude of the acceleration of the particle.

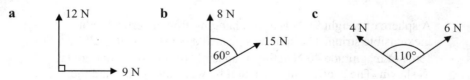

In questions 9 to 15, **i** and **j** are perpendicular unit vectors.

9   A resultant force of $(9\mathbf{i} - 12\mathbf{j})$ N acts on an object of mass 3 kg.

    a   Find the acceleration of the particle in the form $(\lambda\mathbf{i} + \mu\mathbf{j})$.

    b   Find the magnitude of the acceleration.

10 A particle of mass 6 kg with initial velocity $(2\mathbf{i} + \mathbf{j})$ ms^{-1} is acted upon by a resultant force of $(18\mathbf{i} + 3\mathbf{j})$ N.

    a Find the acceleration of the particle in vector form.

    b Find to 3 sf the speed of the particle after 4 seconds.

11 A body of mass 2.4 kg is moving with constant velocity 8 ms^{-1} under the action of three forces $(5\mathbf{i} - 2\mathbf{j})$ N, $(-7\mathbf{i} + 3\mathbf{j})$ N and $(\lambda\mathbf{i} + \mu\mathbf{j})$ N. Find λ and μ.

12 A resultant force $\mathbf{F}$ acts on a particle of mass 5 kg for 3 seconds. During this period the velocity of the particle changes from $(\mathbf{i} - 4\mathbf{j})$ ms^{-1} to $(7\mathbf{i} - 7\mathbf{j})$ ms^{-1}.

    Find $\mathbf{F}$ in vector form.

13 A particle of mass 500 g is acted on by forces of $(-4\mathbf{i} + \mathbf{j})$ N and $(6\mathbf{i} - 6\mathbf{j})$ N.

    a Find to 3 sf the magnitude of the particle's acceleration.

    b Find to the nearest degree the angle this acceleration makes with the vector $\mathbf{j}$.

14 An object of mass 10 kg is subjected to forces $(a\mathbf{i} + 3\mathbf{j})$ N, $(-\mathbf{i} - 17\mathbf{j})$ N and $(12\mathbf{i} + b\mathbf{j})$ N. Given that the object accelerates at 2.5 ms^{-1} in the direction of the vector $(3\mathbf{i} - 4\mathbf{j})$, find the values of a and b.

15 At time $t = 0$ a particle of mass 2 kg is moving with velocity $(3\mathbf{i} + \mathbf{j})$ ms^{-1}. Given that the particle is subject to a resultant force of $(-\mathbf{i} + 4\mathbf{j})$ N, find the time at which the particle is moving parallel to the vector $\mathbf{j}$.

16

    A particle of mass 2.5 kg is at rest on a smooth horizontal plane.
    When a horizontal force F acts on the particle, it accelerates at 3 ms^{-2}.

    Find the magnitude of F.

17 A suitcase of mass 20 kg is pulled along a smooth horizontal surface by a horizontal rope. The suitcase accelerates uniformly at 0.2 ms^{-2}.

    Find the tension in the rope.

18 A car of mass 800 kg on a horizontal road is given a thrust of 4 kN by its engine. Assuming there is no resistance to motion, find the acceleration of the car.

19 A car of mass 1 tonne accelerates uniformly from 20 ms^{-1} to 30 ms^{-1} in 5 seconds on a straight horizontal track. Find the force exerted by the engine during this acceleration assuming there is no resistance to motion.

20 A box of mass 20 kg is pulled along a smooth horizontal plane at a constant speed of 4 ms^{-1} by a force of 30 N inclined at an angle of 20° to the horizontal.

    Find the magnitude of the resistance to motion, giving your answer correct to 3 sf.

21   A car of mass 1200 kg accelerates uniformly from rest to 27 ms^{-1} in 9 seconds along a straight horizontal track. Assuming the car experiences constant resistance to motion of 1800 N, find

    a   the acceleration of the car,

    b   the force exerted by the engine.

    c   Explain why the assumption of constant resistance would not be realistic.

22   A box of mass 4 kg is pulled along a rough horizontal surface by a force of 20 N inclined at an angle of 30° to the horizontal and directed upwards.
The coefficient of friction between the box and the ground is $\frac{1}{\sqrt{3}}$.

    Find the acceleration of the box correct to 2 sf.

23   A particle of mass 3 kg is attached to one end of a light inextensible string which is used to raise and lower the particle. Find to 2 sf the tension in the string when the particle is moving

    a   upwards with acceleration 0.5 ms^{-2},

    b   downwards with acceleration 0.5 ms^{-2},

    c   upwards with constant velocity 3 ms^{-1},

    d   downwards with deceleration 1.5 ms^{-2}.

24   A man of mass 80 kg is in a lift which is accelerating upwards at 2 ms^{-2}.

    a   Find to 2 sf the magnitude of the normal reaction of the floor on the man.

    After a period of motion at constant speed the lift decelerates at 2 ms^{-2}.

    b   Find to 2 sf the magnitude of the normal reaction of the floor of the lift on the man during the period of deceleration.

25   A particle of mass 0.5 kg is placed on a smooth plane inclined at an angle of 30° to the horizontal. Find the acceleration of the particle in terms of g.

26   A girl of mass 30 kg slides from rest down a straight slide of length 4 m inclined at an angle of 35° to the horizontal. Given that the coefficient of friction between the girl and the slide is 0.15, and by modelling the girl as a particle, find to 2 sf

    a   the acceleration of the girl,

    b   the girl's speed at the bottom of the slide.

27   A cyclist accelerates at 1.5 ms^{-2} down a straight road inclined at an angle α to the horizontal without peddling. Given that the cyclist and his bicycle have a total mass of 70 kg and experience constant resistance to motion of 14 N,

    a   find α correct to the nearest degree,

    b   find to 2 sf the magnitude of the normal reaction exerted by the road on the bicycle.

Exercise 11E   Exam Practice

1   A particle of mass 2 kg is acted on by forces $8\mathbf{i}$ N, $(13\mathbf{i} - 6\mathbf{j})$ N and
     $(-7\mathbf{i} + 8\mathbf{j})$ N, where $\mathbf{i}$ and $\mathbf{j}$ are perpendicular unit vectors.

     Find the exact magnitude of the resulting acceleration and the angle it
     makes with the vector $\mathbf{i}$ in degrees correct to 1 decimal place.   **(7 marks)**

2   A man is in a lift of mass 250 kg supported by a light inextensible
     cable. As the lift moves upwards with acceleration 1.3 ms^{-2} it exerts
     a force of magnitude 777 N on the man.

     a   Find the mass of the man.   **(4 marks)**

     b   Find the tension in the lift cable correct to 2 significant figures.   **(4 marks)**

3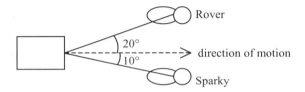

     Two dogs, Rover and Sparky, are pulling a loaded sledge of total mass
     60 kg along smooth horizontal ground. Each dog is attached to the
     sledge by a light inextensible rope. The ropes are horizontal and make
     angles of 20° and 10° respectively with the direction of motion of the
     sledge as shown.

     Given that the sledge experiences a constant resistance to motion of
     100 N and that initially the dogs achieve an acceleration of 1 ms^{-2},
     find the tension in each rope correct to 3 significant figures.   **(9 marks)**

4   A particle is moving on a rough horizontal plane.

     Given that there are no external forces acting on the particle, show
     that it is decelerating at μg ms^{-2}, where μ is the coefficient of friction
     between the particle and the plane.   **(4 marks)**

5   The engine of a car of mass 500 kg cuts out when it is travelling at
     18 ms^{-1} along a straight horizontal road. The driver allows the car to
     come to a halt without applying the brakes.

     In a model of the situation it is assumed that the car is subject to a
     constant resistive force of 400 N. Using this model,

     a   find how long it takes the car to stop,   **(4 marks)**

     b   find how far the car travels before it stops.   **(2 marks)**

     c   Comment on the suitability of the modelling assumption.   **(1 mark)**

6   A child of mass 20 kg travels from rest down a slide inclined at an angle of 40° to the horizontal. When the child has travelled a distance of 2 m her speed is 4.5 ms^{-1}. By modelling the child as a particle, find to 2 significant figures the coefficient of friction between the child and the slide.   **(9 marks)**

7   A body of mass 5 kg is subjected to forces of $(7\mathbf{i} - 2\mathbf{j})$ N, $(-\mathbf{i} + 8\mathbf{j})$ N and $(x\mathbf{i} - \mathbf{j})$ N where $\mathbf{i}$ and $\mathbf{j}$ are perpendicular unit vectors and $x > 0$.

Given that the acceleration produced has magnitude $\sqrt{5}$ ms^{-2}, find the value of x.   **(7 marks)**

8   A particle of mass 500 g is projected vertically upwards from the bottom of a pool of liquid with speed 15 ms^{-1}. As the particle moves in the liquid it is subject to a constant resistive force of magnitude 2.6 N. The particle does not reach the surface of the pool.

a   Find the height the particle reaches above the bottom of the pool.   **(5 marks)**

b   Find to 2 significant figures the speed with which the particle hits the bottom of the pool on its return.   **(4 marks)**

c   Show that the particle takes 2.8 seconds, correct to 2 significant figures, to return to the bottom of the pool.   **(3 marks)**

9

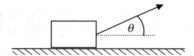

A package of mass 10 kg is pulled along a rough horizontal floor at a constant speed of 0.5 ms^{-1} by a light inextensible rope.
The rope is inclined at an angle θ to the horizontal where $\sin \theta = \frac{5}{13}$.

Given that the coefficient of friction between the package and the floor is $\frac{1}{5}$, find the tension in the rope in terms of g.   **(7 marks)**

10   A particle is placed on a rough horizontal plane inclined at an angle θ to the horizontal. The coefficient of friction between the particle and the plane is μ. Given that the particle begins to move down the slope, show that its acceleration is independent of the mass of the particle and find its magnitude in terms of μ, θ, and g.   **(6 marks)**

11   Sue and her son Oliver are both standing in a lift of mass 250 kg. As the lift moves upwards with uniform acceleration the floor of the lift exerts forces of 621.5 N and 169.5 N respectively on Sue and Oliver. The tension in the cable supporting the lift is 3616 N.

a   Draw a clear diagram showing all the forces acting on the lift.   **(2 marks)**

b   Find the magnitude of the lift's acceleration.   **(4 marks)**

c   Find the mass of Sue and the mass of Oliver.   **(5 marks)**

Connected Particles

Exercise 12S   Skills Practice

1

Two particles A and B, of mass 6 kg and 4 kg respectively, are on a smooth horizontal plane and connected by a light inextensible string.

A horizontal force P is applied to A and when the string is taut the particles move with acceleration 0.5 ms^{-2}.

a Find the tension in the string joining A and B.

b Find the magnitude of P.

2 A car of mass 800 kg is using a chain to tow a trailer of mass 200 kg along a straight horizontal road. The engine of the car produces a driving force of 1.5 kN.

Find the acceleration of the system and the tension in the chain assuming that there is no resistance to motion.

3 A truck of mass 1500 kg is towing a car of mass 750 kg along a straight horizontal road. When the vehicles are accelerating at 4 ms^{-2} the truck and car experience resistances to motion of 2000 N and 800 N respectively.

a Find the tension in the cable joining the vehicles.

b Find the driving force exerted by the car's engine.

4 A van of mass 1 tonne is used to tow a car of mass 600 kg along a straight horizontal road. The vehicles are initially at rest connected by a rope that is taut and the engine of the van produces a driving force of 7 kN. The van and car experience constant resistances to motion of 800 N and 600 N respectively.

a Find the acceleration of the system.

b Find the tension in the rope.

Given that the rope breaks 5 seconds after the vehicles begin moving,

c find to the nearest metre the total distance travelled by the car before it stops.

5 Two particles are connected by a light inextensible string which passes over a smooth pulley. The particles are released from rest. In each case find in terms of g the acceleration of the particles and the tension in the string.

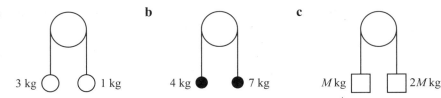

6   Two particles P and Q of mass 5 kg and 2 kg respectively are connected by a light inextensible string which passes over a smooth pulley.
The particles are released from rest.

a   Find the acceleration of P.

When P has travelled 1 metre it hits the ground and does not bounce. Given that in its subsequent motion Q does not hit the pulley,

b   find to 2 sf the greatest height that Q reaches above its original position.

7

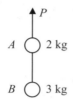

Particle A, of mass 2 kg, is suspended by a string. Particle B, of mass 3 kg, is suspended from A by means of a second string. Both strings are light and inelastic. When a force P is applied vertically upwards to the upper string the particles accelerate upwards at 2.2 ms^{-2}.

a   Find the tension in the string joining the particles.

b   Find the magnitude of P.

8   Two particles are connected by a light inextensible string which passes over a smooth pulley. One particle hangs freely whilst the other is held on a smooth horizontal surface. Find, in terms of g, the acceleration of the system and the tension in the string when the particles are released.

a   6 kg   **b** M kg

2 kg m kg

9   Two particles P and Q of masses 5 kg and 3 kg respectively are connected by a light inextensible string which passes over a smooth pulley.
P is held at rest on a rough horizontal table whilst Q hangs freely.

Given that the coefficient of friction between P and the table is 0.2,

a   find the acceleration of the system in terms of g,

b   find the tension in the string in terms of g.

10   Two particles A and B of masses 6 kg and 2 kg respectively are connected by a light inextensible string which passes over a smooth pulley.
B hangs freely whilst A is held at rest on a rough horizontal table.

Given that when A is released the system remains at rest, find the minimum value of the coefficient of friction between A and the table.

11 A car of mass 1200 kg is towing a trailer of mass 800 kg along a straight horizontal road. The car's engine exerts a driving force of 10 kN and the car and trailer experience resistances to motion of 2400 N and 1600 N respectively.

    a Find the acceleration of the system.

    b Find the tension in the coupling between the car and the trailer.

The car and trailer come to a hill inclined at an angle α to the horizontal where $\sin \alpha = \frac{1}{14}$. Assuming the driving force and resistances to motion remain the same,

    c find the acceleration of the vehicles up the hill.

12

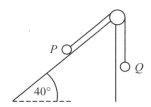

Two particles P and Q of mass 4 kg and 5 kg respectively are connected by a light inextensible string which passes over a smooth pulley. P is held at rest on a smooth plane inclined at an angle of 40° to the horizontal and Q hangs freely.

When P is released, find to 2 sf

    a the acceleration of the system,

    b the tension in the string.

13 Two particles A and B of equal mass are connected by a light inextensible string which passes over a smooth pulley. A is held at rest 1.5 m from the pulley on a smooth plane inclined at an angle of 25° to the horizontal. B hangs freely a distance of 2 m above the ground. Particle A is released.

Find the speed at which A hits the pulley correct to 2 sf.

14 Two particles P and Q of mass 600 g and 800 g respectively are connected by a light inextensible string which passes over a smooth pulley. P is held on a rough plane inclined at an angle of 35° to the horizontal and Q hangs freely. The coefficient of friction between P and the inclined plane is 0.3

The system is released from rest. Find to 2 sf

    a the acceleration of the system,

    b the tension in the string.

15 Two particles A and B of mass 2 kg and 3 kg respectively are connected by a light inextensible string which passes over a smooth pulley. A is held at rest on a rough plane inclined at an angle of 30° to the horizontal and B hangs freely.

When A is released it accelerates at 2.5 ms^{-2}. Find to 2 sf

    a the tension in the string,

    b the coefficient of friction between A and the inclined plane.

Exercise 12E   Exam Practice

1   A recovery vehicle of mass 1 tonne is towing a car of mass 500 kg along a straight horizontal road. The vehicles are accelerating at $0.5\ \mathrm{ms^{-2}}$ and the tension in the tow-bar is 400 N.

Given that the resistance to motion experienced by each vehicle is proportional to its mass, find

  a   the magnitude of the resistance experienced by each vehicle,   **(5 marks)**

  b   the magnitude of the driving force exerted by the engine of the recovery vehicle.   **(3 marks)**

2

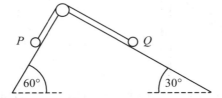

Two particles P and Q of equal mass are connected by a light inelastic string which passes over a smooth pulley. P lies on a rough plane inclined at an angle of 60° to the horizontal and Q lies on a smooth plane inclined at an angle of 30° to the horizontal.

Given that the coefficient of friction between P and the plane it is on is $\frac{1}{\sqrt{3}}$, show that the acceleration of the system when it is released from rest is $\frac{1}{12}g(2\sqrt{3}-3)$.   **(9 marks)**

3

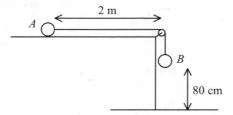

Two particles A and B of mass 600 g and 800 g respectively are connected by a light inextensible string which passes over a smooth pulley. A is held on a smooth horizontal plane a distance of 2 metres from the pulley. B hangs freely a distance of 80 cm above another horizontal plane. The system is released from rest.

  a   Find the tension in the string before B hits the horizontal plane, giving your answer in terms of g.   **(5 marks)**

  b   Find the total time taken for A to reach the pulley correct to 2 significant figures.   **(7 marks)**

  c   Explain how you have used the information that the string is inextensible and the pulley is smooth.   **(2 marks)**

4

Particle A, of mass m_1 kg, is suspended by a string. Particle B, of mass m_2 kg, is suspended from A by means of a second string. The strings are light and inextensible and the particles move upwards under the action of a force of magnitude P N applied vertically upwards to the upper string.

Find an expression in terms of m_1, m_2 and P for the tension in the string joining the particles. **(8 marks)**

5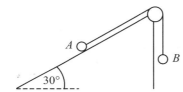

Two particles A and B of mass $3m$ and $2m$ respectively are connected by a light inextensible string which passes over a smooth pulley. A is held at rest on a rough plane inclined at an angle of $30°$ to the horizontal whilst B hangs freely. The coefficient of friction between A and the inclined plane is μ.

Given that when A is released it remains in equilibrium, find the minimum value of μ, giving your answer in the form $k\sqrt{3}$. **(9 marks)**

6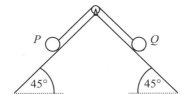

Two particles P and Q, of mass 20 kg and 30 kg respectively, are connected by a light inextensible string passing over a smooth pulley. P and Q are both at rest on rough planes inclined at $45°$ to the horizontal and the string is in a vertical plane containing a line of greatest slope of each plane as shown.

Given that the coefficient of friction between each particle and its respective plane is μ, and both particles are in limiting equilibrium,

a find the value of μ, **(10 marks)**

b show that the force exerted by the string on the pulley has magnitude $24g$ N. **(5 marks)**

7   A car of mass 800 kg is towing a trailer of mass 300 kg up a straight
road inclined at an angle θ to the horizontal where $\sin\theta = \frac{7}{25}$.

The engine produces a driving force of magnitude 5 kN. The car and
trailer experience constant resistances to motion of 1200 N and 500 N
respectively. Find, to an appropriate degree of accuracy,

    a the acceleration of the vehicles,   **(6 marks)**

    b the magnitude of the tension in the tow-bar.   **(4 marks)**

8

                                P Q

Particle P, of mass $3m$ kg is connected to particle Q, of mass m kg,
by a light inextensible string which passes over a smooth pulley.
The particles are released from rest at the same horizontal level,
60 cm above the ground, with the string taut and the hanging parts
of the string vertical.

    a Find the initial acceleration of the system in terms of g.   **(5 marks)**

When P hits the ground it comes immediately to rest.

    b Find the maximum height above the ground reached by Q
assuming that it does not hit the pulley.   **(6 marks)**

9

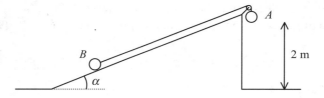

Particle A of mass $3m$ kg is connected to particle B of mass $2m$ kg by
a light inextensible string of length 5 m passing over a small smooth
pulley. B is held at rest on a rough plane inclined at an angle α to the
horizontal where $\sin\alpha = \frac{5}{13}$. The section of string between B and the
pulley is parallel to a line of greatest slope of the plane and the
coefficient of friction between B and the plane is $\frac{11}{36}$. A hangs freely
just below the pulley, a distance of 2 m above horizontal ground.

The system is released from rest.

    a Find the acceleration of the system before A hits the ground,
giving your answer in terms of g.   **(9 marks)**

    b Find the distance of B from the pulley when it comes momentarily
to rest.   **(7 marks)**

Momentum and Impulse

Exercise 13S	Skills Practice

1   Find the magnitude of the momentum of a particle of mass m travelling with speed v if

   a $m = 4$ kg, $v = 5$ ms^{-1} b $m = 12$ kg, $v = 2$ ms^{-1}

   c $m = 500$ g, $v = 4$ ms^{-1} d $m = 600$ g, $v = 18$ kmh^{-1}

2   A particle moving at 1.5 ms^{-1} has momentum of magnitude 6 N s. Find its mass.

3   A particle of mass 2 kg moving with speed 8 ms^{-1} is acted upon by a force which reduces its speed to 5 ms^{-1}. Find the change in momentum of the particle.

4   A golf ball of mass 40 g is at rest when it is struck by a club. Given that the speed of the ball immediately after being struck is 55 ms^{-1}, find the magnitude of the impulse exerted on the ball by the club.

5   A particle of mass 3 kg is moving with speed 2.5 ms^{-1}. The particle receives an impulse in the direction it is moving which increases its speed to 6 ms^{-1}.
   Find the magnitude of the impulse received by the particle.

6   A body of mass 1.5 kg is at rest when it is given an impulse of magnitude 12 N s. Find the speed of the body after receiving the impulse.

7   A snooker ball of mass 0.15 kg hits a cushion on a snooker table at right angles with a speed of 2 ms^{-1} and rebounds with a speed of 1.6 ms^{-1}.

   a   Find the magnitude of the impulse which the cushion exerts on the ball.

   b   State the magnitude of the impulse which the ball exerts on the cushion.

8   A ball of mass 300 g is moving at 5 ms^{-1}. Find the speed of the ball after it receives an impulse of magnitude 0.9 N s in the opposite direction to its motion.

9   Find the magnitude of the impulse received by a box when a force of magnitude 24 N acts on it for 0.2 seconds.

10   A particle of mass 3 kg is travelling at 2 ms^{-1}. A force of magnitude 6 N acts on the particle for 4 seconds in the direction that it is moving.

   a   Find the magnitude of the impulse received by the particle.

   b   Find the speed of the particle after these 4 seconds.

11   A body of mass 4 kg is at rest on a smooth horizontal plane. Find the speed of the body after it is acted on by a horizontal force of magnitude 8 N for 2 seconds.

12 A force of magnitude 2.5 N acts on a particle of mass 800 g which is at rest. Given that after T seconds the particle has speed 5 ms^{-1}, find the value of T.

13 A particle P of mass 3 kg is dropped from a height of 6 m above the ground.

    a Find the speed of P to 2 sf just before it hits the ground.

    The particle bounces and moves vertically upwards with initial speed 7.5 ms^{-1}.

    b Find to 2 sf the magnitude of the impulse exerted on P by the ground.

In questions 14 to 16, **i** and **j** are perpendicular unit vectors.

14 Find to 2 sf the magnitude of the momentum of a particle of mass 2 kg moving with velocity $(3\mathbf{i} - 2\mathbf{j})$ ms^{-1}.

15 A particle of mass 5 kg is moving with a velocity of 6**i** ms^{-1} when it receives an impulse of 10**i** N s. Find the subsequent velocity of the particle.

16 A particle of mass 3 kg is moving with velocity 15**j** ms^{-1}. It is acted on by a constant force, **F** Newtons, for 6 seconds after which its velocity is −5**j** ms^{-1}. Find **F**.

In questions 17 to 24, A and B are particles which are either moving or at rest on a smooth horizontal surface.

17 A has mass 2 kg and is moving with speed 4 ms^{-1} when it collides directly with B which has mass 1 kg and is at rest. After the collision A has speed 2 ms^{-1} and its direction of motion is unchanged. Find the speed of B after the collision.

18 A has mass 3 kg and moves with speed 4 ms^{-1}. B has mass 2 kg and is at rest. A collides directly with B and as a result of the collision A and B coalesce. Find the speed of the new particle formed in the collision.

19 A has mass 1.5 kg and is moving at 4 ms^{-1} when it collides directly with B which has mass 3 kg and is moving in the same direction at 1 ms^{-1}. As a result of the collision A comes to rest. Find the speed of B after the collision.

20 A and B have masses 0.5 kg and 0.2 kg respectively. They are moving in the same direction with speeds of 5 ms^{-1} and 2 ms^{-1} respectively when they collide directly. After the collision A continues to move in the same direction with speed 4 ms^{-1}. Find the speed of B after the collision.

21 A and B have masses 300 g and 200 g respectively. The particles are moving towards each other with speeds of 2.5 ms^{-1} and 5 ms^{-1} respectively when they collide directly. After the collision, the direction of motion of both particles is reversed and B has speed 2 ms^{-1}.

    a Find the speed of A after the collision.

    b Find the magnitude of the impulse exerted on A by B.

22 A has mass 0.8 kg and is moving with speed v ms^{-1}. B has mass 0.3 kg and is moving in the opposite direction to A with speed $2v$ ms^{-1}. The particles collide directly and coalesce.

Given that the combined particle moves with speed 2 ms^{-1} in the direction that A was moving before the collision, find the value of v.

23 A and B have masses 4 kg and 3 kg respectively. They are moving towards each other with speeds of $2u$ ms^{-1} and $3u$ ms^{-1} respectively when they collide directly. After the collision, B has reversed its direction of motion and is travelling with speed u ms^{-1}.

Find the speed and direction of motion of A after the collision.

24 A and B have masses $4m$ kg and m kg respectively and move towards each other with speeds of 1 ms^{-1} and 3 ms^{-1} respectively. The particles collide directly and after the collision the direction of motion of B is reversed and it has speed 2 ms^{-1}.

a Find the speed and direction of motion of A after the collision.

b Find, in terms of m, the magnitude of the impulse exerted by B on A.

25 A railway truck of mass 35 tonnes travelling at 4 ms^{-1} collides with a stationary truck of mass 40 tonnes. As a result of the collision, the trucks couple together. By modelling the trucks as particles, find their common speed after the collision, giving your answer correct to 3 sf.

26 Two particles P and Q, of masses 1 kg and 0.5 kg respectively, are connected by a light inextensible string. Initially P and Q are at rest on a smooth horizontal plane and the string is slack. P is projected away from Q horizontally with speed 3 ms^{-1}.

a Find the speed of the particles after the string becomes taut.

b Find the magnitude of the impulse exerted on P as a result of the string becoming taut.

27 A bullet of mass 30 g is moving horizontally with speed 500 ms^{-1} when it hits a wall. The bullet comes to rest in 0.01 seconds, becoming embedded in the wall.

a Find the magnitude of the impulse exerted on the bullet by the wall.

b Find the magnitude of the resistive force exerted by the wall on the bullet, assuming that it is constant.

28 A block of mass 4 kg is dropped from a height of 3 m above the ground. When it hits the ground, it sinks in a distance of 2 cm before coming to rest. Find to 2 sf

a the magnitude of the impulse exerted by the block on the ground,

b the magnitude of the resistive force exerted by the ground on the block, assuming that it is constant.

Exercise 13E	Exam Practice

1   Two balls A and B of mass 0.3 kg and 0.4 kg respectively are moving in opposite directions on a smooth horizontal plane when they collide directly. Immediately before colliding the balls have speeds of 3 ms^{-1} and 2 ms^{-1} respectively. After the collision the direction of motion of each particle is reversed and the speed of B is twice the speed of A.

    a Find B's speed immediately after the collision. **(4 marks)**

    b Find the magnitude of the impulse exerted on B in the collision. **(3 marks)**

2   A gun of mass 4 kg fires a bullet of mass 40 g and recoils with initial speed 4.5 ms^{-1}. The bullet hits a vertical wall and travels a further 2 m before coming to rest. Assuming that the bullet travels horizontally and with constant speed before hitting the wall, and that the wall exerts a constant resistive force in bringing the bullet to rest, find

    a the magnitude of the impulse exerted by the wall on the bullet, **(4 marks)**

    b the magnitude of the resistive force. **(4 marks)**

3   Particle P, of mass 5 kg, and particle Q, of mass 8 kg, are projected vertically upwards from horizontal ground at the same time.
The impulses given to the two particles are of magnitude 98 Ns and 147 Ns respectively.

    Find which particle returns to ground level first and how much longer it takes for the second particle to return to ground level. **(8 marks)**

4   A railway truck, of mass 2000 kg, collides with another truck, of mass 1800 kg, moving in the same direction on a straight horizontal track. The speeds of the trucks immediately before they collide are 4 ms^{-1} and 1.5 ms^{-1} respectively. When the trucks collide they couple and move together under the action of a constant resistive force. Given that the trucks come to a halt 20 seconds after the collison,

    a find the magnitude of the resistance to motion, **(6 marks)**

    b find to 3 significant figures the distance the trucks travel after the collision. **(2 marks)**

5   Particle A, of mass 5 kg, is moving with speed 16 ms^{-1} on a smooth horizontal plane when it collides directly with particle B which is at rest. The particles coalesce and move together with speed V ms^{-1}.

    The combined particle then collides directly with particle C, of mass 4 kg, which is moving in the same direction with speed 4 ms^{-1}.

    Given that these particles also coalesce and move with speed 8 ms^{-1}, find the mass of particle B and the value of V. **(8 marks)**

6 A ball of mass 500 g is dropped from a height of 2.5 m above horizontal ground.

    a Find the speed of the ball just before it hits the ground. **(3 marks)**

The ball bounces and moves vertically upwards reaching a height of 1 metre above the ground.

    b Find the magnitude of the impulse exerted by the ball on the ground, giving your answer correct to 2 significant figures. **(5 marks)**

7 A toy car of mass 150 g is designed to split into two parts, the larger of which has mass 100 g. When the car is travelling at 4 ms^{-1} it splits and the larger part continues to move in the same direction whilst the smaller part moves in the opposite direction.

Given that the speed, v ms^{-1}, of the larger part is twice the speed of the smaller part after the split, find the value of v. **(5 marks)**

8 Particle A, of mass m kg, and particle B, of mass km kg, are moving in opposite directions on a smooth horizontal table when they collide directly. Immediately before the collision A has speed $3u$ ms^{-1} and B has speed u ms^{-1}. After the collision, the direction in which each particle is moving is reversed and the speed of each particle is halved.

    a Find the value of k. **(4 marks)**

    b Find, in terms of m and u, the magnitude of the impulse exerted on B in the collision. **(3 marks)**

9 A boy of mass 60 kg stands in a lift of mass 750 kg which is supported by a light inextensible wire. When the lift is accelerating upwards the tension in the wire is 10 370 N.

Find to an appropriate degree of accuracy

    a the acceleration of the system, **(3 marks)**

    b the force that the lift floor exerts on the boy. **(3 marks)**

The lift accelerates from rest but after 4 seconds the wire snaps. A safety cable prevents the lift from falling more than 50 cm below its level at the instant the wire snapped. Using the modelling assumption that the safety cable is inextensible,

    c find the magnitude of the impulse exerted by the cable on the lift, giving your answer correct to 2 significant figures. **(6 marks)**

In a more refined model it is assumed that rather than being inextensible, the safety cable would take 0.1 seconds to stop the lift after it had fallen to 50 cm below its level when the wire snapped.

    d Using this model, find to 2 significant figures the magnitude of the force that the safety cable exerts on the lift in bringing it to rest, assuming that this force is constant. **(3 marks)**

Dynamics Review

| Exercise 14E   Exam Practice |

1

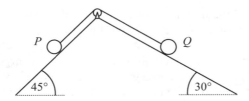

Two particles P and Q, of mass 4 kg and 5 kg respectively, are connected by a light inextensible string passing over a smooth pulley. Particles P and Q lie on smooth planes inclined at 45° and 30° to the horizontal respectively with the string in a vertical plane containing a line of greatest slope of each plane. The system is released from rest.

Find the direction in which particle P moves and the magnitude of its acceleration correct to 2 significant figures.   **(8 marks)**

2   An iron bucket of mass 5 kg falls from rest from the roof of a house and travels 12 m before hitting the ground. The base of the bucket is horizontal when it lands and sinks 3 cm into the ground.

Modelling the bucket as a particle and assuming that the resistive force exerted by the ground on the bucket is constant,

a   find the magnitude of the resistive force exerted by the ground, giving your answer in terms of g.   **(8 marks)**

b   Explain how the resistive force would in fact vary as the bucket sinks into the ground.   **(2 marks)**

3

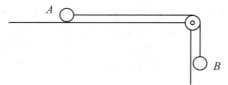

Particles A and B, of equal mass m kg, are connected by a light inextensible string which passes over a smooth pulley. A lies on a rough horizontal plane and B hangs freely as shown.
The coefficient of friction between A and the plane is μ.

a   Show that when the system is released from rest the tension in the string is given by $\frac{1}{2}mg(\mu + 1)$ N.   **(7 marks)**

Given that initially A is a distance d metres from the pulley,

b   find an expression in terms of d, g and μ for the speed at which A is travelling when it hits the pulley.   **(5 marks)**

4   Two balls A and B are moving in the same direction along a horizontal
straight line with speeds of 3 ms^{-1} and 1.5 ms^{-1} respectively when they
collide. After the collision both particles continue to move in the same
direction with A having speed 2.5 ms^{-1}. Given that the mass of A is
four times the mass of B,

    a   find the speed of B immediately after the collision.   **(4 marks)**

    Given also that the impulse exerted on A in the collision is of
magnitude 2 Ns,

    b   find the mass of A.   **(3 marks)**

5   A particle of mass 4 kg is subjected to forces of $(9\mathbf{i} - 2\mathbf{j})$ N,
$(-3\mathbf{i} + 19\mathbf{j})$ N and $(2\mathbf{i} + p\mathbf{j})$ N, where $\mathbf{i}$ and $\mathbf{j}$ are perpendicular unit
vectors, producing an acceleration of $(q\mathbf{i} + 3\mathbf{j})$ ms^{-2}.

    Find the values of the constants p and q.   **(6 marks)**

6

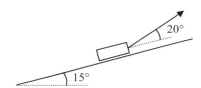

    A boy is using a rope to try and pull a sledge of mass 4 kg up an icy
slope inclined at an angle of 15° to the horizontal. The rope is in the
same vertical plane as a line of greatest slope and makes an angle of
20° with it as shown.

    In a model of the situation it is assumed that the slope is smooth, the
rope is inextensible and the sledge is treated as a particle.

    a   Use this model to find the tension in the rope when the sledge is
at rest, giving your answer correct to 2 significant figures.   **(3 marks)**

    b   Comment on the suitability of the modelling assumptions used.   **(3 marks)**

    In a more refined model it is assumed that the coefficient of friction
between the sledge and the slope is 0.08

    c   Use this model to find correct to 2 significant figures the
acceleration of the sledge when the tension in the rope is 16 N.   **(7 marks)**

7   Particle A, of mass 500 g, and particle B, of mass 600 g are at rest
3 metres apart on a rough horizontal plane. At the same time, both
particles are given an impulse of magnitude 6 Ns in the direction $\overrightarrow{AB}$.
The coefficient of friction between each particle and the plane is 0.2

    Find, to the nearest metre,

    a   the distance that B would travel if it was not hit by particle A,   **(7 marks)**

    b   the distance that B travels before it is hit by A.   **(8 marks)**

8   A film director wishes to shoot a scene in which a valuable statue of mass 20 kg descends 60 m to the ground in a lift. The lift accelerates uniformly from rest for 7.5 seconds at which time the cable supporting the lift snaps and the lift falls freely to the ground. Given that during the initial acceleration the statue exerts a force of 180 N on the floor of the lift,

   a   find the speed of the lift when the cable snaps,   **(5 marks)**

   b   find to an appropriate degree of accuracy the speed at which the lift hits the ground.   **(5 marks)**

9

Particle B, of mass 3 kg, is suspended from particle A, of mass 7 kg, by means of a light inextensible string.

Given that the particles accelerate upwards when a force of magnitude P N is applied vertically upwards to particle A, find an inequality which must be satisfied by P.   **(7 marks)**

10   A particle of mass 5 kg is moving with uniform velocity $(6\mathbf{i} + 3\mathbf{j})$ ms^{-1}, where $\mathbf{i}$ and $\mathbf{j}$ are perpendicular unit vectors.

Find the speed of the particle after it is subjected to a resultant force of $(\mathbf{i} - 4\mathbf{j})$ N for 10 seconds, giving your answer correct to 3 significant figures.   **(6 marks)**

11   A particle of mass 2 kg is released from rest on a rough plane inclined at an angle of $60°$ to the horizontal. The coefficient of friction between the particle and the plane is 0.4

   a   Show that the acceleration of the particle is $\frac{1}{10}g(5\sqrt{3} - 2)$.   **(5 marks)**

   Find to 2 significant figures

   b   how long it takes the particle to travel 15 metres down the slope,   **(3 marks)**

   c   the speed of the particle when it has travelled 15 metres.   **(2 marks)**

12   A boy uses a catapult to fire a stone of mass 100 g vertically upwards with initial speed 25 ms^{-1}. The stone travels 10 m before hitting a horizontal branch. It then travels 2.5 cm vertically into the branch.

Assuming that the resistive force applied to the stone by the branch is constant, find its magnitude correct to 2 significant figures.   **(7 marks)**

13

Particles P and Q have masses m_1 kg and m_2 kg respectively where $m_1 < m_2$. They are connected by a light inextensible string which passes over a smooth pulley. The particles are released from rest with the string taut and the hanging parts of the string vertical.

a   Find the magnitude of the acceleration of the particles in terms of m_1, m_2 and g.   **(5 marks)**

b   Show that the tension in the string is $\dfrac{2m_1m_2g}{m_1+m_2}$ N.   **(3 marks)**

c   State how you have used the fact that the pulley is smooth.   **(1 mark)**

14   Two balls A and B of mass m kg and $2m$ kg respectively are moving towards each other on a smooth horizontal plane when they collide directly. Immediately before the collision A has speed 4.5 ms^{-1} and B has speed 1 ms^{-1}. After the collision the direction of motion of B is reversed.

B then collides directly with ball C, of mass $3m$ kg, which is at rest. After this collision B is at rest and C moves with speed 1.2 ms^{-1}.

Find the speed and direction of motion of A after the first collision.   **(8 marks)**

15

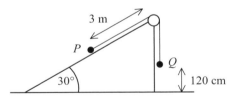

Two particles P and Q of mass 3 kg and 5 kg respectively are connected by a light inextensible string passing over a smooth pulley. P is held at rest a distance of 3 metres from the pulley on a rough plane inclined at an angle of 30° to the horizontal. Q hangs freely a distance of 1.2 metres above a horizontal plane. The section of string between P and the pulley is parallel to a line of greatest slope of the inclined plane.

When P is released, Q takes 0.85 seconds to reach the horizontal plane where it comes instantly to rest.

a   Find the coefficient of friction between P and the inclined plane, giving your answer correct to 2 significant figures.   **(10 marks)**

b   Find, to the nearest cm, the total distance travelled by P before it first comes to rest.   **(7 marks)**

Moments

1   Each force shown is acting in the plane of a lamina containing the point O.
Find the exact magnitude of the moment of each force about O and state its sense.

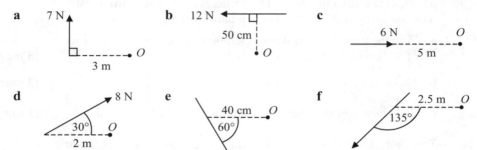

2   A force of magnitude 6 N exerts a clockwise moment of 9 Nm about a point P.
Find the perpendicular distance between P and the line of action of the force.

3   A force of magnitude F N exerts an anticlockwise moment of 15 Nm about a
point P. Given that the perpendicular distance between P and the line of action of
the force is 120 cm, find the value of F.

4   The forces acting on a light rod are shown. Each force acts at right angles to the
length of the rod. Find in each case the total moment about the point O on the rod
and its sense.

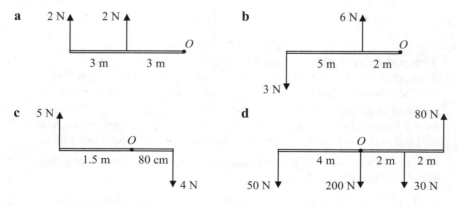

5   A light rod PQ has length 4 metres. A force of magnitude 2 N is applied to the
rod at P acting perpendicular to the length of the rod. Another force of magnitude
5 N is applied to the rod at a point d m from P acting parallel to the first force.

Given that the total moment about the point Q on the rod is 20 Nm, find d.

6 The forces shown act in the plane of a lamina containing the point O. Find, to 3 sf if appropriate, the total moment about the point O on the lamina and its sense.

a

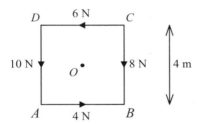

3 m, 4 m, 8 N, 7 N, O

b

2.5 N, 5 m, 4 N, 40°, O

7 $ABCD$ is a square lamina of side 4 metres whose centre is the point O. Forces of magnitude 4 N, 8 N, 6 N and 10 N act in the directions $\overrightarrow{AB}$, $\overrightarrow{CB}$, $\overrightarrow{CD}$ and $\overrightarrow{DA}$ respectively as shown.

D — 6 N — C
10 N — O — 8 N — 4 m
A — 4 N — B

Find the magnitude and sense of the total moment of these forces about

a the point A, **b** the point O.

8 A light rod is in equilibrium under the action of forces acting perpendicular to its length. Find the magnitude of each unknown force.

a
R
2 m, 2 m
50 N, S

b
F
2 m, 4 m
10 N, H

c X, Y
3 m, 4 m
70 N

d Q
3 m, 2 m, 5 m
P, 300 N

9 A light rod is in equilibrium under the action of forces acting perpendicular to its length. Find the distance x in each case.

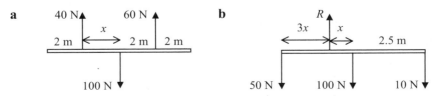

a 40 N, 60 N, x, 2 m, 2 m, 2 m, 100 N

b R, $3x$, x, 2.5 m, 50 N, 100 N, 10 N

10   A uniform rod AB of length 6 metres and mass 20 kg rests on a support at the point C where $AC = 2$ metres. A particle is attached to the rod at A so that the rod is in equilibrium in a horizontal position.

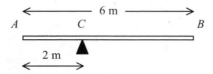

a   Draw a diagram showing all the forces acting on the rod.

b   Find the mass of the particle.

c   Find, in terms of g, the magnitude of the reaction on the rod at C.

11   A uniform rod PQ has length 3 m and weight 150 N. The rod rests in equilibrium in a horizontal position on two supports, one at P and the other 0.5 m from Q.

Find the magnitude of the reaction on the rod at each of the supports.

12   Two children of mass 40 kg and 35 kg sit at either end of a see-saw which is pivoted in the middle and of length 6 metres. A third child of mass 30 kg sits on the see-saw at a point such that it is in equilibrium in a horizontal position.

a   Suggest suitable models for the children and for the see-saw.

b   Find the distance of the third child from the pivot.

13   A non-uniform rod AB of length 12 metres and mass 30 kg rests in a horizontal position on a support at its midpoint. When a particle of mass 24 kg is attached to the rod at A and a particle of mass 36 kg is attached at B the rod is in equilibrium.

Find the distance of the centre of mass of the rod from A.

14   A uniform rod XY of length 8 metres and weight 60 N has loads of weight 80 N and 100 N attached at X and Y respectively. Find the distance from X at which a support should be placed so that the rod is in equilibrium when it is horizontal.

15

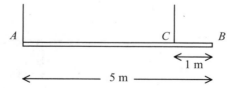

A uniform rod AB of length 5 metres and mass M kg is suspended in a horizontal position by two vertical strings. One of the strings is attached at A and the other is attached at C, 1 metre from B. The tension in the string attached at A is $9g$ N.

a   Draw a diagram showing all the forces acting on the rod.

b   Find in terms of g the tension in the string attached at C.

c   Find M.

16

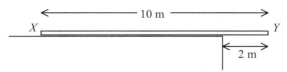

A uniform plank XY of length 10 m and weight 560 N rests on a horizontal roof which Y overhangs by 2 m. A man of weight 1400 N walks from X towards Y.

a Find the distance of the man from X when the plank is on the point of tilting.

When a load of weight W N is placed on the plank at X the man is able to walk to Y without the plank tilting.

b Find the minimum value of W.

17 Two acrobats stand at the two ends of a uniform beam AB of length 6 metres and mass 50 kg. The acrobat at A has mass 45 kg and the acrobat at B has mass 60 kg. The beam rests on a support 1 m from A and on another support 1 m from B.

a Find to 2 sf the magnitude of the reaction on the beam at each of the supports.

b State how you have used the fact that the beam is uniform.

18

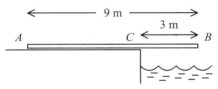

A uniform plank AB has length 9 m and mass 20 kg. The plank overhangs a pier as shown with the point C at the edge of the pier where $BC = 3$ m. A child of mass 30 kg stands on the plank at A while her father walks along the plank to the point B. When he reaches B, the plank is on the point of tilting about C.

a Find, in terms of g, the magnitude of the reaction on the plank at C when the father reaches B.

b Find the mass of the father.

19

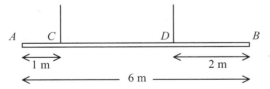

A uniform beam AB of length 6 metres and weight 180 N is suspended in a horizontal position by two vertical strings. The strings are attached at the points C and D on the beam where $AC = 1$ metre, and $DB = 2$ metres.

a Find the tension in each of the strings.

When a load of weight W is attached to the beam at B, it is on the point of tilting.

b State the tension in the string attached at C.

c Find the tension in the string attached at D and the value of W.

Exercise 15E   Exam Practice

1

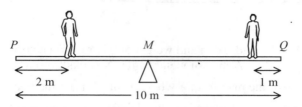

A non-uniform plank PQ has length 10 metres and mass 25 kg. The plank is smoothly supported at its midpoint, M. A man of mass 60 kg stands on the plank at a distance of 2 metres from P and another man stands on the plank at a distance of 1 metre from Q.

Given that the plank is in equilibrium in a horizontal position with the reaction on the plank at M having magnitude 1372 N, find the distance of the centre of mass of the plank from P. **(6 marks)**

2

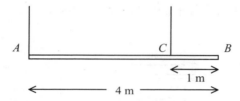

A plank AB, of uniform cross-section, has length 4 m and mass 25 kg. The plank is suspended by two vertical ropes attached at A and at the point C, 1 m from B. A particle of mass 15 kg is placed on the plank 30 cm from B and a particle of mass 10 kg is placed on the plank between A and C. The plank is in equilibrium in a horizontal position with the tension in the rope attached at C four times the tension in the rope attached at A.

a   Suggest a suitable model for the plank. **(1 mark)**

b   Find, in terms of g, the tension in the rope attached at C. **(3 marks)**

c   Find the distance between the two particles. **(5 marks)**

3

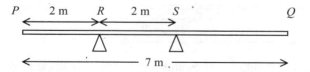

A uniform plank PQ of length 7 metres and weight 420 N is smoothly supported at the points R and S, where $PR = RS = 2$ metres. When Amy stands on the plank at P, it is on the point of tilting.

a   Find Amy's weight. **(4 marks)**

b   Find how far Amy can walk along the plank without it tilting. **(4 marks)**

4

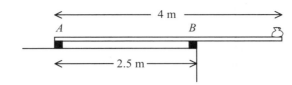

Tony sees a bag on the end of a plank overhanging a swimming pool. The plank is 4 m long and rests in a horizontal position on two bricks. Brick A is positioned under one end of the plank and brick B is at the edge of the pool, 2.5 m away. Tony steps on the plank at A and tries to walk along the plank to reach the bag. Tony has mass 70 kg, the plank has mass 30 kg and the bag has mass 4 kg.

a Suggest a suitable model for the plank.   **(1 mark)**

By modelling the bricks as smooth supports,

b find, to the nearest cm, how far Tony can walk along the plank before it is on the point of tilting.   **(5 marks)**

Tony places a load of mass m on the plank at A. He is then able to walk to the other end of the plank without it tilting.

c Find the minimum value of m.   **(3 marks)**

5   A uniform rod XY of length 6 metres and mass 20 kg is suspended in a horizontal position by vertical ropes attached at X and Y. A load of mass 6 kg is attached to the rod 2 metres from X and the rod remains in equilibrium.

a Suggest suitable models for

    i   the ropes,
    ii the 6 kg load.   **(2 marks)**

b Find, in terms of g, the tension in each rope.   **(6 marks)**

c Explain how you have used the fact that the rod is uniform.   **(1 mark)**

6

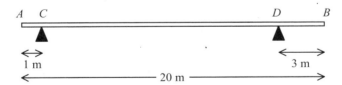

A uniform beam AB of mass 30 kg and length 20 metres rests in a horizontal position on two smooth supports at C and D where $AC = 1$ metre and $DB = 3$ metres. A man of mass 70 kg stands on the beam at A and a woman of mass 60 kg stands on the beam at D.

Given that the plank is in equilibrium, find the magnitude of the force exerted on the plank by the supports at C and D, giving your answers correct to 2 significant figures.   **(6 marks)**

7   A non-uniform rod PQ of length 5 metres and mass 6 kg is smoothly supported at the point R where $PR = 2.1$ metres.

A load of weight 8.4 N is attached to the rod at P and the rod rests in equilibrium in a horizontal position.

Find the distance of the centre of mass of the rod from P.   **(4 marks)**

8

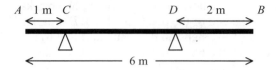

A uniform beam AB of length 6 metres and mass 30 kg is smoothly supported at C, 1 metre from A and at D, 2 metres from B.
Daniel, of mass 60 kg, stands on the beam 2 metres from A and Jack, of mass 75 kg, stands on the beam a distance of x metres from B.
The beam is in equilibrium in a horizontal position and the reaction on the beam at D is 50% greater than the reaction on the beam at C.

a   Find to 2 significant figures the magnitude of the reaction at

i C,
ii D.   **(4 marks)**

b   Find the value of x.   **(5 marks)**

9

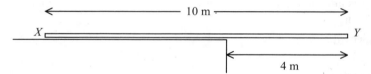

A non-uniform plank XY of length 10 metres and mass 40 kg rests on a horizontal table with the end Y projecting 4 metres over the edge of the table as shown. When a package of mass 25 kg is placed on the plank 1 metre from X and a package of mass 90 kg is placed on the plank 1.5 metres from Y the plank is in limiting equilibrium.

By modelling the packages as particles and the plank as a non-uniform rod,

a   find the distance of the centre of mass of the plank from X,   **(5 marks)**

b   find the magnitude of the force which the edge of the table exerts on the plank, giving your answer in terms of g.   **(2 marks)**

The 25 kg package is removed and the 90 kg package is moved so that the plank is again in limiting equilibrium.

c   Find to the nearest cm how far the 90 kg package is from Y.   **(3 marks)**

d   State how you have used the modelling assumption that the plank is a rod.   **(1 mark)**

Course Review

Exercise 16E   Exam Practice

1 A stone is dropped from the top of a cliff. One second later another stone is thrown vertically downwards from the same point with speed 12 ms^{-1}. The stones land at the bottom of the cliff at the same time.

   a Find the height of the cliff correct to the nearest metre. **(7 marks)**

   b State a modelling assumption that you used in your calculation and comment on its suitability. **(2 marks)**

2 Particle P, of mass 3 kg, is travelling with speed 4 ms^{-1} on a rough horizontal plane when it collides directly with particle Q, of mass 2 kg, which is stationary. After the collision, Q moves with speed 4 ms^{-1}.

   a Find the speed of P after the collision. **(3 marks)**

   b Find the magnitude of the impulse exerted on Q by P. **(2 marks)**

Following the collision, Q comes to rest after travelling a distance of 3 metres.

   c Find to an appropriate degree of accuracy the coefficient of friction between Q and the plane. **(6 marks)**

3

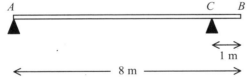

A uniform beam AB has length 8 metres and weight 400 N. The beam rests in a horizontal position on two smooth supports at A and C, where $CB = 1$ metre. Two friends Liam and Trent, each of weight 600 N, stand on the beam such that Liam is half as far as Trent is from B. The beam is in equilibrium and the ratio of the magnitude of the reaction on the beam at A to that at C is 1 : 3

Find to the nearest centimetre how far Trent is from B. **(7 marks)**

4 John and Sandra have their radio-controlled cars in a car park. They stand together with John's car 1 metre west of them and Sandra's car 42 metres north and 31 metres west of them. John sets his car travelling at a constant velocity of $(-3\mathbf{i} + 6\mathbf{j}) \text{ ms}^{-1}$ where $\mathbf{i}$ and $\mathbf{j}$ are unit vectors due east and north respectively. Two seconds later, Sandra sets her car travelling with constant velocity $(5\mathbf{i} - 4\mathbf{j}) \text{ ms}^{-1}$.

Show that the two cars collide, and find the distance of the crash from John and Sandra. **(9 marks)**

5

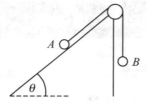

Two particles A and B have masses 4 kg and m kg respectively and are connected by a light inextensible string which passes over a smooth pulley. A lies at rest on a rough plane inclined at an angle θ to the horizontal, where $\sin \theta = \frac{3}{5}$, and B hangs freely. The string is in a vertical plane containing a line of greatest slope of the inclined plane.

Given that the coefficient of friction between A and the inclined plane is $\frac{1}{2}$, and that the system is in equilibrium,

a   show that the minimum value of m is $\frac{4}{5}$,   **(8 marks)**

b   find the maximum value of m.   **(5 marks)**

6   The position vector, **r** cm, of a particle at time t seconds, relative to a fixed origin O is given by

$$\mathbf{r} = (t-1)\mathbf{i} + (3t-1)\mathbf{j}$$

where **i** and **j** are perpendicular unit vectors.

a   Find the value of t for which the particle is closest to O.   **(6 marks)**

b   Find the least distance of the particle from O, giving your answer correct to 2 significant figures.   **(3 marks)**

7

Alan

30°

Bhavin

20°

Carlos

Three workers at a zoo, Alan, Bhavin and Carlos, are pulling a bear of mass $\frac{1}{2}$ tonne in a cage of mass 200 kg along horizontal ground at constant speed. Each worker pulls a horizontal rope and the cage moves in the direction that Bhavin is pulling. Alan's and Carlos's ropes make angles of 30° and 20° with Bhavin's rope as shown. The coefficient of friction between the cage and the ground is $\frac{1}{20}$.

Given that the tension in Bhavin's rope is 50% greater than the tension in Alan's rope, find to 2 significant figures the tension in each of the three ropes.   **(11 marks)**

8   A car travelling at U ms^{-1} accelerates uniformly at 0.2 ms^{-2} until its speed has increased by 10 ms^{-1}.

    a   Find the time taken for this increase in speed.   **(2 marks)**

    Given that the car travels 1.5 km whilst accelerating,

    b   find U.   **(4 marks)**

9

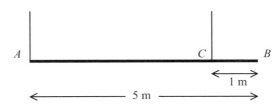

A uniform rod AB has length 5 metres and mass 15 kg.

The rod is suspended in a horizontal position by vertical light inextensible strings attached at A and at C, 1 metre from B.

    a   Find the maximum mass which can be attached to the rod at B such that the rod remains in equilibrium.   **(4 marks)**

    b   Find, to 2 significant figures, the tension in the rope attached at C in this situation.   **(2 marks)**

10   In a model of a pile driver, the "pile" is regarded as a cylindrical rod of mass 250 kg. This is knocked into the ground by dropping a "driver", of mass 1000 kg, from rest at a point 2.5 metres vertically above the pile. When the driver hits the pile it is assumed that they move together as a single body.

    a   Find the speed of the driver just before it hits the pile.   **(3 marks)**

    b   Find the common speed of the pile and driver immediately after the impact.   **(3 marks)**

    The ground is assumed to exert a constant resistive force in bringing the system to rest. Given that the pile travels 20 cm into the ground,

    c   find the magnitude of the resistive force exerted by the ground, giving your answer correct to an appropriate degree of accuracy.   **(5 marks)**

11   The resultant $\mathbf{R}$ of two forces $\mathbf{F}_1$ and $\mathbf{F}_2$ is $(5\mathbf{i} - 6\mathbf{j})$ N where $\mathbf{i}$ and $\mathbf{j}$ are perpendicular unit vectors.

    a   Find the magnitude of $\mathbf{R}$ in newtons to 1 decimal place.   **(2 marks)**

    b   Find to the nearest degree the angle $\mathbf{R}$ makes with the vector $\mathbf{i}$.   **(2 marks)**

    Given that $\mathbf{F}_1$ acts in a direction parallel to the vector $(2\mathbf{i} - 3\mathbf{j})$ and that $\mathbf{F}_2$ acts in a direction parallel to the vector $(-\mathbf{i} + 2\mathbf{j})$,

    c   find $\mathbf{F}_1$ and $\mathbf{F}_2$.   **(5 marks)**

12

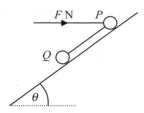

Two particles P and Q, of mass 3 kg and 8 kg respectively, are connected by a light inextensible string. They are placed on a rough plane inclined at an angle θ to the horizontal, where $\sin \theta = 0.6$ A horizontal force of magnitude F N acts on P which is higher up the plane than Q. The string is parallel to a line of greatest slope of the plane. The coefficient of friction between each particle and the plane is 0.4 and the particles are on the point of sliding down the plane.

a   Find, in terms of g, the tension in the string joining the particles.   **(6 marks)**

b   Find the value of F correct to 2 significant figures.   **(8 marks)**

13   Particle A, of mass 300 g, is moving with speed 4 ms^{-1} on a smooth horizontal table when it collides directly with particle B, of mass 500 g, which is at rest. The two particles coalesce and move as a single particle, C. This particle then bounces at right angles against a vertical wall, receiving an impulse of magnitude 1.6 Ns.

Find the speed of C after it bounces against the wall.   **(6 marks)**

14

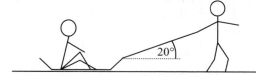

Richard is pulling his friend Roger along rough horizontal ground on a toboggan by means of a light inextensible string which makes an angle of 20° with the horizontal. Roger and the toboggan have a combined mass of 35 kg and are moving in a straight line with constant speed.

Given that the coefficient of friction between the toboggan and the ground is 0.15, find to 2 significant figures the tension in the string.   **(7 marks)**

15   A car is travelling at a constant speed of 102 kmh^{-1} along a straight horizontal road. Ahead of the car is a van travelling at a constant speed of 54 kmh^{-1} in the same direction.

a   Show that 102 kmh^{-1} can be expressed as $28\frac{1}{3}$ ms^{-1}.   **(2 marks)**

Given that the car is capable of a maximum deceleration of 5 ms^{-2}, and assuming that the van continues to move with constant speed,

b   find how close the car can get to the van before braking if the vehicles are not to collide.   **(8 marks)**

16 A uniform rod AB has length 6 metres and mass 12 kg. Loads of mass 8 kg and 16 kg are suspended from the rod at A and B respectively. The rod is smoothly supported by a pivot at the point P so that it rests in horizontal equilibrium.

    a Find the magnitude of the force exerted on the rod by the pivot, giving your answer in terms of g. **(2 marks)**

    b Find the distance AP. **(4 marks)**

    c Explain how you have used the fact that the rod is uniform. **(1 mark)**

17

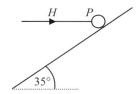

A particle P, of mass 3 kg, is held at rest on a rough plane inclined at an angle of 35° to the horizontal by the action of a force H. H acts horizontally towards the plane and is in the same vertical plane as a line of greatest slope.

Given that when $H = 45$ N, P is on the point of moving up the slope,

    a show that the coefficient of friction between P and the plane is 0.40 correct to 2 significant figures, **(7 marks)**

    b find the value of H, correct to 2 significant figures, when P is on the point of moving down the slope. **(6 marks)**

18

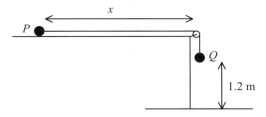

Two particles P and Q of masses m kg and $2m$ kg respectively are connected by a light inextensible string which passes over a smooth pulley. P is held at rest on a rough horizontal plane a distance x from the pulley. Q hangs freely 1.2 metres above a horizontal floor. The coefficient of friction between P and the plane it is on is 0.25

The system is released from rest.

    a Find the acceleration of P in terms of g. **(7 marks)**

    b Find to 2 significant figures the speed with which Q hits the floor. **(3 marks)**

When Q hits the floor, it does not rebound.
Given that P does not hit the pulley,

    c find the minimum value of x. **(6 marks)**

19 A car is moving along a straight road at a constant speed of 24 ms^{-1} when the driver sees a fallen tree blocking the road 50 metres ahead. The car is capable of decelerating at a maximum rate of 6 ms^{-2}.

In an initial model of the situation, the car is assumed to decelerate at its maximum rate as soon as the driver sees the tree.

Using this model,

    a find how long it takes the car to come to rest, **(2 marks)**

    b find how far the car is from the tree when it comes to rest. **(3 marks)**

In a more refined model it is assumed that the driver does not react immediately and that the car decelerates at its maximum rate from a time 0.25 seconds after the driver sees the tree.

    c Find the speed with which the car hits the tree according to this model, giving your answer correct to 2 significant figures. **(4 marks)**

    d Write down two further considerations which a more sophisticated model might include. **(2 marks)**

20

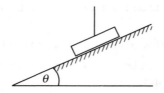

A loaded sledge of total mass 150 kg lies on a rough plane inclined at an angle θ to the horizontal where $\sin \theta = \frac{7}{25}$. The sledge is held at rest on the point of sliding down the slope by a vertical light inextensible string. Given that the sledge is subject to a frictional force of magnitude 131.6 N,

    a find the tension in the vertical string. **(5 marks)**

    b find the coefficient of friction between the sledge and the slope. **(5 marks)**

21 A particle of mass 0.5 kg is subjected to two forces, $F_1 = (5i + 2j)$ N and $F_2 = (\lambda i + \mu j)$ N, where i and j are perpendicular unit vectors and λ and μ are constants. The resultant of the two forces is R.

Given that R is parallel to the vector $(2i - j)$,

    a find to the nearest degree the angle between R and the vector i, **(2 marks)**

    b show that $\lambda + 2\mu + 9 = 0$. **(4 marks)**

Given also that $\lambda = 1$,

    c find the magnitude of the acceleration of the particle, giving your answer in the form $k\sqrt{5}$. **(6 marks)**

22

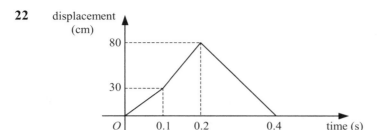

The displacement-time graph shows the motion of a steel ball of mass 50 g along a straight line on a pinball table. From its initial position the ball travels 30 cm in 0.1 seconds. The ball then receives an impulse and travels 50 cm in the same direction in a further 0.1 seconds. The ball then receives a second impulse and returns to its original position in 0.2 seconds. In each period of motion the ball moves with constant velocity.

Find the magnitude of the impulse exerted on the ball

a   after 0.1 seconds,   **(4 marks)**

b   after 0.2 seconds.   **(3 marks)**

23   Three forces $(2\mathbf{i} - 7\mathbf{j})$ N, $(p\mathbf{i} - 3\mathbf{j})$ N and $(q\mathbf{i} - 2p\mathbf{j})$ N act on a particle.

Given that the particle is in equilibrium, find the values of the constants p and q.   **(4 marks)**

24

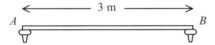

A uniform shelf of mass 3 kg and length 3 m rests in a horizontal position on two smooth brackets at A and B. A tin of mass 600 g is placed on the shelf a distance of 50 cm from B.

a   Suggest suitable models for the shelf and the tin.   **(2 marks)**

b   Find, in terms of g, the magnitude of the force exerted on the shelf by the bracket at B.   **(4 marks)**

25   A bucket of sand of total mass 40 kg is being lifted from rest on the ground by a crane on a building site. The tension in the cable attached to the bucket is 412 N until, after 8 seconds, the cable snaps and the bucket falls to the ground.

a   Find to 3 significant figures the total time for which the bucket is in the air.   **(11 marks)**

The bucket hits the ground with its base level and comes to rest in 0.01 seconds under the action of a constant resistive force.

b   Find to the nearest cm the depth to which the bucket is buried.   **(4 marks)**

26   An underground train travels on a straight horizontal track between two stations A and B which are 1.2 km apart. The train accelerates from rest at A at a constant rate of 0.5 ms^{-2} until it reaches a speed of $V \text{ ms}^{-1}$. It maintains this speed until it decelerates uniformly at 1 ms^{-2}, coming to rest at B.

    a   Illustrate the train's journey on a velocity-time graph.   **(2 marks)**

    b   Find, in terms of V, the length of time for which the train was accelerating.   **(2 marks)**

    Given that the train travels from A to B in a total time of $1\frac{1}{2}$ minutes,

    c   show that $V^2 - 60V + 800 = 0$,   **(5 marks)**

    d   find V, making your reasoning clear.   **(3 marks)**

27   A car of mass 1250 kg is towing a caravan of mass 750 kg along a straight horizontal road. The resistance to motion experienced by each vehicle is proportional to its mass. Given that the total resistance to motion experienced by the car and caravan is 16 kN,

    a   find the resistance to motion experienced by the car.   **(2 marks)**

    Given also that the car's engine is producing a driving force of 20 kN,

    b   find the acceleration of the system,   **(3 marks)**

    c   find the tension in the coupling between the vehicles.   **(3 marks)**

    The car and caravan ascend a hill inclined at an angle α to the horizontal. The driving force and resistances to motion are unchanged. Given that the vehicles move up the hill with constant velocity,

    d   find α correct to the nearest degree.   **(4 marks)**

28

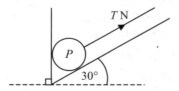

A particle P, of mass 5 kg, is at rest against a smooth vertical plane and a smooth plane inclined at an angle of 30° to the horizontal. The two planes meet in a horizontal line. P is also held by a light inextensible string which is parallel to a line of greatest slope of the inclined plane. The tension in the string is T N.

Denoting the reaction on P from the inclined plane by R and the reaction on P from the vertical plane by R_V, show that

    a $T = 10g - \sqrt{3}\,R$,   **(4 marks)**

    b $2T = 5g - \sqrt{3}\,R_V$,   **(3 marks)**

    c $R_V = 2R - 5\sqrt{3}\,g$.   **(3 marks)**

29 A diver of mass 65 kg is being lowered into the sea in a submersible capsule suspended by a cable. The empty capsule has mass 150 kg. As the capsule accelerates downwards, the water exerts a constant resistive force of magnitude 100 N on it and the diver experiences a constant reaction of 572 N from the floor of the capsule.

    a Find the magnitude of the acceleration of the capsule. **(3 marks)**

    b Find the tension in the cable correct to 2 significant figures. **(3 marks)**

30 Duncan and Simon are skateboarding in an empty warehouse. Relative to a door O, at time $t = 0$, Duncan is at the point with position vector $(3\mathbf{i} + 18\mathbf{j})$ m and Simon is at the point with position vector $(14\mathbf{i} + 10\mathbf{j})$ m, where $\mathbf{i}$ and $\mathbf{j}$ are unit vectors parallel to the walls of the building. Duncan is travelling with constant velocity $(4\mathbf{i} - 2\mathbf{j})$ ms^{-1} and Simon is travelling with constant velocity $(3\mathbf{i} - \mathbf{j})$ ms^{-1}.

    a Find the position vector of Simon at time t seconds. **(2 marks)**

    At time $t = 5$, Simon passes through the point P.

    b Show that Duncan also passes through the point P and find the value of t when this occurs. **(6 marks)**

    c Find, to 2 significant figures, the least distance between the two skateboarders in their subsequent motion. **(8 marks)**

31

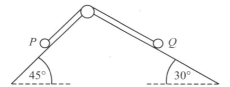

Two particles P and Q are connected by a light inextensible string which passes over a smooth pulley. P lies on a smooth plane inclined at an angle of $45°$ to the horizontal and Q lies on a smooth plane inclined at an angle of $30°$ to the horizontal. The string is in a vertical plane containing a line of greatest slope of each inclined plane.

Given that the particles do not move when released from rest, show that the ratio of the mass of P to the mass of Q is $1 : \sqrt{2}$ **(7 marks)**

32 Two particles P and Q are released from rest at the same horizontal level on a rough plane inclined at an angle θ to the horizontal. The coefficients of friction between the particles and the plane are μ_P and μ_Q respectively. Given that both particles travel the same distance to the bottom of the slope but that P takes one-third of the time taken by Q, show that

$$\mu_Q = \tfrac{1}{9} (\mu_P + 8 \tan \theta).$$ **(12 marks)**

Answers

Exercise 1S   Skills Practice

1 **a** 10   **b** 21   **c** 6
   d 65   **e** 22.9   **f** 5.4

2 60 m

3 8.4 ms^{-1}

4 **a** −3   **b** 10   **c** 6
   d 5   **e** 28   **f** 7

5 3.4 ms^{-2}

6 96 m

7 4.5 s, 40.5 m

8 **a** 15 ms^{-1} **b** 0.5 ms^{-2} **c** 175 m

9 1.5 ms^{-2}, 40 s

10 **a** 7 ms^{-1} **b** 24 ms^{-1}

11 0.18 ms^{-2}, 10449 m

12 **b** 1.5 s

13 **b** $2u + 5a = 20$ **c** $u = 5, a = 2$

14 **a** 4 ms^{-2} **b** 30 ms^{-1}
    c 3.5 s   **d** 112.5 m

Exercise 1E   Exam Practice

1 **a** 6 ms^{-2} **b** 19 ms^{-1}

2 $x = 150$, 50 ms^{-1}

3 $S = 143, T = 13$

4 **a** 3 ms^{-1} **b** 0.75 m

5 **a** 7 s   **b** 113.75 m

6 **a** 52 m   **b** 4.74 s (3 sf)

Exercise 2S   Skills Practice

1 **b** 6 kmh^{-1} **c** 4.5 kmh^{-1}

2 **a** 3 ms^{-2} **b** 2 ms^{-2} **c** 156 m

3 **b** 14 ms^{-1} **c** 2 ms^{-1}

4 **b** 3 s   **c** 6 ms^{-2}

5 **b** 810 m   **c** 18 ms^{-1}

6 **a** e.g.
   OA – constant vel. away from start pt.
   AB – stationary
   BD – constant vel. back to start pt.,
       then away from it in other direction
   b 5 ms^{-1} **c** −300 m   **d** 4.8 ms^{-1}

7 **b** 10.5   **c** 121 m

8 **b** 67.5   **c** 2700 m

Exercise 2E   Exam Practice

1 **b** 11 ms^{-1}

2 **b** 0.54 ms^{-2} (2 sf)

3 **a** 2 ms^{-2} **b** 16

4 **b** 1.5 ms^{-2} **c** 311 m

Exercise 3S   Skills Practice

1 7 ms^{-1}

2 3.5 s

3 **a** particle as it is small   **b** 16 m
   c e.g. air reistance, actual accel. less

4 10 m

5 28 ms^{-1}

6 **a** 2.4 s   **b** 25 ms^{-1}

7 **a** 390 m   **b** 16 s

8 8.9 m

Exercise 3E   Exam Practice

1 **a** 2 s   **b** marble – particle,
                 motion freely under gravity

2 5 s

5 **b** 2.7 s (2 sf)

6 1 : 2

7 83 s (nearest second)

Exercise 4E   Exam Practice

1 5 s

2 **a** 1.2 ms^{-2} **b** 19 : 25

3 **b** 24 ms^{-1}

4 **a** 4 s   **b** 39 m (2 sf)

5 3 ms^{-1}

6 **a** 0.6 ms^{-2} **b** 45   **c** 34.3 (3 sf)

7 15 s

8 **a** −6 ms^{-2}, 75 ms^{-1} **c** 937.5 m

9 **b** 2 mins   **c** 3240 kmh^{-2} **d** 0.25 ms^{-2}

10 **b** 6

11 1 s

12 **a** 120 m

Exercise 5S   Skills Practice

1 **a** m   **b** 2n   **c** m + n
     d m + 2n   **e** −n   **f** m − n

2 **a** 2p   **b** $^1/_2$q   **c** p + q
     d p + $^1/_2$q   **e** −2p   **f** −$^1/_2$q
     g −p − q   **h** q − p   **i** 2p + $^1/_2$q
     j p − $^1/_2$q   **k** 2p − q   **l** $^1/_2$q − 2p

3 **a** 50 km, 016°   **b** 403 km, 263°
     c 51.1 m, 119°   **d** 12.6 km, 063°

4 **a** 6i + 4j   **b** 7i + j
     c 17i + 4j   **d** 14i − 9j

5 **a** 5   **b** 13   **c** 6.08   **d** 11.2

6 ± 15

7 **a** 45.0°   **b** 33.7°   **c** 6.3°   **d** 66.8°

8 **a** 12i − 16j   **b** $^7/_5$i + $^{24}/_5$j

9 **a** $^1/_5$(3i + 4j)   **b** $^1/_{25}$(7i − 24j)
     c $^{\sqrt2}/_2$(i − j)   **d** $^1/_5$(−√5 i + 2√5 j)

10 5

11 **a** $^1/_3$ **b** −$^1/_2$

12 **a** 5   **b** −$^1/_9$

13 **a** 5√3 i + 5j   **b** −5i
     c 8√2 i − 8√2 j   **d** −15i − 15√3 j

Exercise 6S   Skills Practice

1 **a** 4i ms^{-1} **b** (9i − 12j) ms^{-1}
     c (−$^5/_2$i + 6j) ms^{-1}

2 **a** 3i   **b** 2i − j   **c** i + 4j
     d 2i + 3j   **e** −2i − 4j   **f** 3i + $^{11}/_2$j

3 3.61 ms^{-1}

4 **a** 5.39 ms^{-1} **b** 68°

5 (6i + 3j) m

6 **a** 2i + 4j   **b** 5i − 4j   **c** 8i + 6j
     d 5i + 5j   **e** 7i + 3j   **f** −i

7 (12i − 9j) m

8 (−17i + 12j) m

9 **a** $^1/_2$i   **b** 2j   **c** i − 2j
     d 3i − 2j   **e** −2i + 2j   **f** $^1/_2$i + 4j

10 (i + $^{12}/_5$j) ms^{-1}

11 **a** 5i   **b** 2i + 6j   **c** i − 7j
     d 4i + 11j   **e** −i + 4j   **f** $^{15}/_2$i − $^1/_2$j

12 3.25 ms^{-1}, 157°

13 13.0 ms^{-1}

14 **a** (2ti + 3tj) m   **b** 2 s

15 **a** [(3 + t)i + 2tj] m
     b [(3 + t)i + (2t − 2)j] m
     c (8i + 10j) m

16 **a** [(t + 1)i + (t − 1)j] m   **c** 4 s, 2.8 m

17 **a** [3ti + (6 − 4t)j] m
     b [(2t + 3)i − 2tj] m
     c 3 s, (9i − 6j) m

18 **a** A [2ti + tj] m,
       B [(3t − 4)i + (20 − 4t)j] m
     b 4 s
     c 2 m

19 **b** 3 s   **c** 3.5 s

Exercise 6E   Exam Practice

1 **a** −35   **b** $(^2/_5\mathbf{i} - {}^{14}/_5\mathbf{j})$ ms^{-2}
     c 82° (nearest degree)

2 **a** $(-5\mathbf{i} + 10\mathbf{j})$ kmh^{-1}
     b $[(5 - 5h)\mathbf{i} + (10h - 16)\mathbf{j}]$ km
     c 9$\mathbf{j}$ km
     d 10.30 a.m.

3 $^{13}/_{17}(15\mathbf{i} - 8\mathbf{j})$ ms^{-1}

4 **a** Alex $[8t\mathbf{i} + (20t - 200)\mathbf{j}]$ m
      Sally $[(10t - 300)\mathbf{i} + (22t - 350)\mathbf{j}]$ m
     b 106 m (nearest m), 2:31:52.5

5 **a** $(^3/_4\mathbf{i} + \mathbf{j})$ ms^{-1} **b** 6.3 m (2 sf)

6 **a** 1, 5   **b** 2, 0 m

7 **b** $[(t - 384)\mathbf{i} + (348 - t)\mathbf{j}]$ m   **d** 1.04 pm

8 **a** $[(14 - 2t)\mathbf{i} + (t + 2)\mathbf{j}]$ m   **b** 4 s

9 **a** $[(2h + 24)\mathbf{i} + (13h - 29)\mathbf{j}]$ km
     b $[(4h - 24)\mathbf{i} + (32 - 4h)\mathbf{j}]$ km
     d 5.7 km (2 sf)

10 **a** $(-11\mathbf{i} + 19\mathbf{j})$ ms^{-1}
      b 30° (nearest degree)

11 **a** $[(8t - 38)\mathbf{i} + (-t - 2)\mathbf{j}]$ cm
      b $13t^2 - 282t + 1549$ **c** 9

Exercise 7S   Skills Practice

1 **a** 13 N, 023°   **b** 50 N, 143°
     c 17.9 N, 333°   **d** 25 N, 016°
     e 125 N, 331°   **f** 3.16 N, 198°

2 **a** 17 N, 088°   **b** 9.64 N, 339°
     c 13.0 N, 151°

3 **a** $(-3\mathbf{i} - 10\mathbf{j})$ N   **b** 0   **c** $(^7/_2\mathbf{i} - {}^3/_4\mathbf{j})$ N

4 **a** $\lambda = 1, \mu = 1$ **b** $\lambda = 2, \mu = -3$
     c $\lambda = 2, \mu = -1$

5 −8

6 50 N, 73.7°

7 **a** $(9\mathbf{i} - 2\mathbf{j})$ N   **b** 9.2 N   **c** 13°

8 3

9 3, 7

10   horiz.   vert.
     a $7\cos 20°$ N, $7\sin 20°$ N
     b $4\cos 70°$ N, $4\sin 70°$ N
     c $5\cos 45°$ N, $5\sin 45°$ N
     d $3\cos 30°$ N, $3\sin 30°$ N
     e $8\cos 30°$ N, $-8\sin 30°$ N
     f $R\cos\theta$ N, $R\sin\theta$ N

11 **a** $12\sin 30°$ N   **b** $8\sin 45°$ N
      c $4\cos 60°$ N

12   parallel   perp.
     a 0 N,   10 N
     b 3.42 N,   9.40 N
     c 10.4 N,   6 N
     d 10 N,   17.3 N
     e 14.8 N,   2.60 N
     f 5.66 N,   5.66 N

13 **a** 17.2 N, 31.5°   **b** 20.0 N, 61.9°
      c 2.73 N, 172°   **d** 5.68 N, 42.8°

14 22.0

Exercise 8S   Skills Practice

1 **a** $P = 15\sqrt3$ N, $Q = 15$ N
     b $P = 5\sqrt3$ N, $Q = 10$ N
     c $P = (6\sqrt3 - 6)$ N, $Q = 6\sqrt6$ N
     d $P = (5\sqrt2 - 4)$ N, $Q = (4\sqrt2 - 5)$ N

2 **a** 10 N, 36.9°   **b** $7\sqrt3$ or 12.1 N, 30°
     c 15.8 N, 26.2°   **d** 19.2 N, 36.4°

3 $\lambda = 2, \mu = 1$

4 $\lambda = -3, \mu = 2$

5 6.4 N, 39°

6 −3, 2

7 **b** weight = 2g N, reaction = 2g N

8 **b** weight = 0.4g, tension = 0.4g

9 **b** 46.2 N   **c** 23.1 N

10 **a** 29.8 N   **b** 4.0 kg

11 **a** 7.8 N   **b** 23°

12 **a** $F = 10$ N, $R = 32$ N
      b $F = 10.4$ N, $R = 36$ N

13 **a** 10 N   **b** 20 N

14 **a** 8.3 N   **b** 9.1 N

15 13 N, 7.4 N

Exercise 8E   Exam Practice

1   15 N, 127° (nearest degree)

3    $X = 129$, $Y = 142$

4   42° (nearest degree)

5   39500 N, 39400 N

6   54 N (2 sf)

7    $\mathbf{F}_2 = (7\mathbf{i} - 14\mathbf{j})$ N, $\mathbf{F}_3 = (-10\mathbf{i} + 15\mathbf{j})$ N

8   a 60°   b 150 N (2 sf)

Exercise 9S   Skills Practice

2   a $2g$ N   b 12 N

3    $^4/_5$

4   a not moving, in limiting equilibrium
     b moving
     c not moving, not in limiting equilibrium
     d not moving, in limiting equilibrium

5   a $5g$ N   b $6g$ N

6   a $4\sqrt{3}$ N   b 4 N   c $^1/_{\sqrt{3}}$

7   27°

8   0.20

9   0.27

10   a $10\sqrt{2}$ N   b $20\sqrt{2}$ N

Exercise 9E   Exam Practice

1    $^4/_5$

2   0.41 (2 sf)

3   1200 N (2 sf)

4   150 N (2 sf)

5   0.26 (2 sf)

8   0.71

Exercise 10E   Exam Practice

1   −2

2   a 23.5 N (3 sf)   b 15.1 N (3 sf)

3   a $^{96}/_5 g$ b $^{28}/_5 g$

4   530 N (2 sf)

5    $\frac{10\sqrt{2}g}{3}$

6    $\dfrac{g}{\sqrt{3}+1}$, $\dfrac{g}{\sqrt{2}(\sqrt{3}+1)}$

7    $X/_{mg}$

9    $^7/_{10}$, $^3/_2$

11   3.2 N, 3.6 N

12   $(118 - 10\sqrt{3})$ N

Exercise 11S   Skills Practice

1   6 N

2   18 ms^{-2}

3   5 kg

4   7.2 ms^{-2}

5   a 4 ms^{-2} b 12 ms^{-1}

6   a 4 ms^{-2} b 40.5 m

7   1.35 s

8   a 3 ms^{-2} b 4.04 ms^{-2} c 1.19 ms^{-2}

9   a $(3\mathbf{i} - 4\mathbf{j})$ ms^{-2} b 5 ms^{-2}

10   a $(3\mathbf{i} + ^1/_2\mathbf{j})$ ms^{-2} b 14.3 ms^{-1}

11   $\lambda = 2$, $\mu = -1$

12   $(10\mathbf{i} - 5\mathbf{j})$ N

13   a 10.8 ms^{-2} b 158°

14   $a = 4$, $b = -6$

15   6 s

16   7.5 N

17   4 N

18   5 ms^{-2}

19   2000 N

20   28.2 N

21   a 3 ms^{-2} b 5400 N
     c e.g. resistance would vary with speed

22   0.12 ms^{-2}

23   a 31 N   b 28 N   c 29 N   d 34N

24   a 940 N   b 620 N

25   $^1/_2 g$

26   a 4.4 ms^{-2} b 5.9 ms^{-1}

27   a 10°   b 680 N

Exercise 11E   Exam Practice

1 $5\sqrt{2}$ ms^{-2}, 8.1° (1 dp)

2 **a** 70 kg   **b** 3600 N (2 sf)

3 55.6 N, 109 N (3 sf)

5 **a** 22.5 s   **b** 202.5 m
   c e.g. not very suitable as resistance
          would decrease with speed

6 0.16 (2 sf)

7 4

8 **a** 7.5 m   **b** 8.3 ms^{-1} (2 sf)

9 $2g$ N

10 $g(\sin\theta - \mu\cos\theta)$

11 **b** 1.5 ms^{-2} **c** Sue: 55 kg, Oliver: 15 kg

Exercise 12S   Skills Practice

1 **a** 2 N   **b** 5 N

2 1.5 ms^{-2}, 300 N

3 **a** 3800 N   **b** 11800 N

4 **a** 3.5 ms^{-2} **b** 2700 N   **c** 197 m

5 **a** $\frac{1}{2}g$, $\frac{3}{2}g$ N   **b** $\frac{3}{11}g$, $\frac{56}{11}g$ N
   c $\frac{1}{3}g$, $\frac{4}{3}Mg$ N

6 **a** $\frac{3}{7}g$ or 4.2 ms^{-2} **b** 1.4 m

7 **a** 36 N   **b** 60 N

8 **a** $\frac{1}{4}g$, $\frac{3}{2}g$ N   **b** $\frac{mg}{m+M}$, $\frac{mMg}{m+M}$ N

9 **a** $\frac{1}{4}g$ **b** $\frac{9}{4}g$ N

10 $\frac{1}{3}$

11 **a** 3 ms^{-2} **b** 4000 N   **c** 2.3 ms^{-2}

12 **a** 2.6 ms^{-2} **b** 36 N

13 2.9 ms^{-1}

14 **a** 2.2 ms^{-2} **b** 6.1 N

15 **a** 22 N   **b** 0.42

Exercise 12E   Exam Practice

1 **a** 300 N, 150 N   **b** 1200 N

3 **a** $\frac{12}{35}g$ N   **b** 0.94 s (2 sf)
   c string – accel. same for both particles
       pulley – tension same either side

4 $\frac{m_2 P}{m_1+m_2}$ N

5 $\frac{1}{9}\sqrt{3}$

6 **a** $\frac{1}{5}$

7 **a** 0.26 ms^{-2} (2 sf)   **b** 1400 N

8 **a** $\frac{1}{2}g$ **b** 1.5 m

9 **a** $\frac{1}{3}g$ **b** 2 m

Exercise 13S   Skills Practice

1 **a** 20 Ns   **b** 24 Ns   **c** 2 Ns   **d** 3 Ns

2 4 kg

3 6 Ns (loss)

4 2.2 Ns

5 10.5 Ns

6 8 ms^{-1}

7 **a** 0.54 Ns   **b** 0.54 Ns

8 2 ms^{-1}

9 4.8 Ns

10 **a** 24 Ns   **b** 10 ms^{-1}

11 4 ms^{-1}

12 1.6

13 **a** 11 ms^{-1} **b** 55 Ns

14 7.2 Ns

15 8**i** ms^{-1}

16 −10**j** N

17 4 ms^{-1}

18 2.4 ms^{-1}

19 3 ms^{-1}

20 4.5 ms^{-1}

21 a $^{13}/_6$ ms^{-1} b 1.4 Ns

22 11

23 u ms^{-1}, direction reversed

24 a 0.25 ms^{-1}, direction reversed   b 5m Ns

25 1.87 ms^{-1}

26 a 2 ms^{-1} b 1 Ns

27 a 15 Ns   b 1500 N

28 a 31 Ns   b 5900 N

Exercise 13E   Exam Practice

1 a 0.4 ms^{-1} b 0.96 Ns

2 a 18 Ns   b 2025 N

3 Q, 0.25 s

4 a 535 N   b 28.2 m (3 sf)

5 3 kg, 10

6 a 7 ms^{-1} b 5.7 Ns (2 sf)

7 8

8 a 3   b $^9/_2$ mu Ns

9 a 3.0 ms^{-2} (2 sf)   b 770 N (2 sf)
   c 10 000 Ns (2 sf)   d 110 000 N (2 sf)

Exercise 14E   Exam Practice

1 down slope, 0.36 ms^{-2} (2 sf)

2 a 2005g N   b e.g. initially greater,
      reducing as bucket's speed decreases

3 b $\sqrt{dg(1-\mu)}$ ms^{-1}

4 a 3.5 ms^{-1} b 4 kg

5 $p = -5$, $q = 2$

6 a 11 N (2 sf)
   b e.g. smooth – reasonable as icy
            inextensible – probably reasonable
            particle – makes little difference
   c 0.57 ms^{-2} (2 sf)

7 a 26 m (nearest m)   b 13 m (nearest m)

8 a 6 ms^{-1} b 28 ms^{-1} (2 sf)

9 $P > 98$

10 9.43 ms^{-1}

---

11 b 2.1 s (2 sf)   c 14 ms^{-1} (2 sf)

12 860 N (2 sf)

13 a $\dfrac{(m_2 - m_1)g}{m_1 + m_2}$ c tension same either side

14 1.1 ms^{-1}, direction reversed

15 a 0.30 (2 sf)   b 1.73 m (nearest cm)

Exercise 15S   Skills Practice

1 a 21 Nm, clock.   b 6 Nm, anti.
   c 0   d 8 Nm, clock.
   e √3 Nm, anti.   f 25√2 Nm, anti.

2 1.5 m

3 12.5

4 a 18 Nm, clock.   b 9 Nm, anti.
   c 10.7 Nm, clock.   d 460 Nm, anti.

5 1.6

6 a 4 Nm, anti.   b 3.28 Nm, clock.

7 a 8 Nm, clock.   b 24 Nm, anti.

8 a $R = 100$ N, $S = 50$ N
   b $F = 15$ N, $H = 5$ N
   c $X = 40$ N, $Y = 30$ N
   d $P = 200$ N, $Q = 500$ N

9 a 3 m   b 62.5 cm

10 b 10 kg   c 30g N

11 90 N, 60 N

12 a children – particles,
      see-saw – uniform rod
   b 0.5 m

13 3.6 m

14 $4^1/_3$ m

15 b 15g N   c 24

16 a 9.2 m   b 140 N

17 a 650 N, 870 N
   b weight acts at midpoint

18 a 120g N   b 70 kg

19 a 60 N, 120 N   b 0   c 270 N, 90 N

Exercise 15E   Exam Practice

1   3.4 m

2   **a** uniform rod   **b** 40g N   **c** 2.25 m

3   **a** 315 N   **b** $4^2/_3$ m

4   **a** uniform rod   **b** 2.63 m (nearest cm)
   c 38.4 kg

5   **a i** inextensible string   **ii** particle
   b 14g N, 12g N
   c weight acts at midpoint

6   C : 860 N, D : 710 N (2 sf)

7   2.4 m

8   **a i** 650 N (2 sf)   **ii** 970 N (2 sf)   **b** 2.64

9   **a** -3.5 m   **b** 155g N
   c 2.89 m (nearest cm)   **d** it is straight

Exercise 16E   Exam Practice

1   **a** 51 m (nearest m)
   b e.g. no air resistance,
        reasonable as stones small

2   **a** $^4/_3$ ms^{-1} **b** 8 Ns   **c** 0.27 (2 sf)

3   3.11 m (nearest cm)

4   34 m

5   **b** 4

6   **a** $^2/_5$ **b** 0.63 cm (2 sf)

7   A : 92 N, B : 140 N, C : 130 N (2 sf)

8   **a** 50 s   **b** 25

9   **a** 22.5 kg   **b** 370 N (2 sf)

10 **a** 7 ms^{-1} **b** 5.6 ms^{-1}
    c 110 000 N (2 sf)

11 **a** 7.8 N (1 dp)   **b** 50° (nearest degree)
    c $F_1 = (8\mathbf{i} - 12\mathbf{j})$ N, $F_2 = (-3\mathbf{i} + 6\mathbf{j})$ N

12 **a** $^{56}/_{25}g$ N   **b** 29 N (2 sf)

13 0.5 ms^{-1}

14 52 N (2 sf)

15 **b** $17^7/_9$ m

16 **a** 36g N   **b** $3^2/_3$ m
    c weight acts at midpoint

17 **b** 6.9 N

18 **a** $^7/_{12}g$ **b** 3.7 ms^{-1} (2 sf)   **c** 4 m

19 **a** 4 s   **b** 2 m   **c** 6.9 ms^{-1}
    d e.g. decel. takes time to reach max.
        air resistance

20 **a** 1000 N   **b** $^7/_{24}$ or 0.29 (2 sf)

21 **a** 27° (nearest degree)   **c** 6√5 ms^{-2}

22 **a** 0.1 Ns   **b** 0.45 Ns

23 $p = -5, q = 3$

24 **a** shelf – uniform rod, tin – particle
    b 2g N

25 **a** 10.3 s (3 sf)   **b** 9 cm (nearest cm)

26 **b** 2V s   **d** 20

27 **a** 10 000 N   **b** 2 ms^{-2} **c** 7500 N
    d 12° (nearest degree)

29 **a** 1 ms^{-2} **b** 1900 N (2 sf)

30 **a** $[(3t + 14)\mathbf{i} + (10 - t)\mathbf{j}]$ m
    b 6.5 s   **c** 2.1 m (2 sf)